BAPTISTS
and the
AMERICAN
REVOLUTION

How God's People *Shaped* the Course of our Nation

CALEB GARRAWAY

Baptists and the American Revolution

Remnant Publishing
Copyright © 2014 Caleb Garraway
ISBN: 978-0-9914963-2-7

REMNANT MINISTRIES
215 S. Marion Avenue
Washington, IA 52353

www.remnantministriesonline.com
917.412.0059

Proofread and edited by Katie Garraway.

Front Cover Painting — *The Battle of Bunker Hill: the patriots await the British assault,* by Don Troiani.

Back Cover Paintings — *The Lexington Green* by Don Troiani (top) and *The Nation Makers* by Howard Pyle (bottom).

All rights reserved. No part of this publication may be reproduced, stored in a retrieval system, or transmitted in any form or by any means – electronic, mechanical, photocopy, recording, or any other – except for brief quotations in printed reviews, without the prior permission of Remnant Ministries and/or Caleb Garraway.

TABLE OF CONTENTS

Foreword 5
Introduction 7
A Brief Background 9
Setting the Example 15
Advocates of Liberty 45
The Highest of Commendations 75
The Formulation of National Documents 79
The Danbury Baptists 89
Conclusion 99
Endnotes 101
What We Believe 107
About the Author 127

The Meeting House which John Hart built for the Baptist Church of Hopewell N.J.

John Hart Speaker

COPIED BY PERMISSION OF Wm BROTHERHEAD.

FOREWORD

In the Bible, Joshua was concerned that the next generation would forget their heritage. He was concerned that they would forget all that God had done for the children of Israel. So he commanded for twelve stones to be brought up out of the Jordan River. These stones represented to the next generation what God had done and could do in the lives of His people. Oh if only we, today, would pick up the stones of our Baptist history and look back and say, *"If God could do it then, it can be done in my generation!"*

Today, the church has been weakened by apathy and ignorance: apathy regarding their Baptist heritage and ignorance about what it really is! This timely book reminds us of our strong history and the influence that Baptists had in the founding of this nation. We recognize that not of all of our founders were Bible-believing Christians, but it is certainly accurate to say that most were greatly influenced by Christian leaders (*many* of them being Baptists) and most assuredly by and through the prayers of the people of God.

At the founding of our nation, brave men stood against wicked tyranny. They stood before the powerful nation of Great Britain and declared independence, proclaiming, *"We have no king but King Jesus!"* The time may come once again for the people of God to stand against tyranny and proclaim our independence from the enemies of freedom and liberty!

I am thankful for the testimony of my dear friend, Caleb Garraway. There are many evangelists in our country – but few have the talent, a commitment to excellence, and a genuine walk with God that Caleb has. I encourage you to dive into this book and be encouraged as I have been by the wonderful heritage we have as Baptists!

- Pastor William Tyson
Woodlawn Baptist Church
Bowie, MD
www.wbcbowie.org

INTRODUCTION

The period of American history surrounding and including the War for Independence has always been most fascinating to me. Long have I desired further study on the particular influence of our Baptist heritage throughout our nation's inception. *Baptists and the American Revolution* was inspired and birthed through my delighted discovery of a book similarly titled, compiled by William Cathcart and published 100 years after our Founding Fathers signed the Declaration of Independence. Cathcart (1826-1908) was one of the premier Baptist historians of the 19th century and greatly helped in the documentation of our Bible-believing heritage. His book is no longer in copyright; and unfortunately, very few have even heard of its existence.

In the following pages and chapters, I have taken the liberty of using the premise of Cathcart's original work, but have added numerous pages filled with many pertinent details and fascinating stories based on my studies of other historical sources. This collaboration has resulted in a book quite different from the first of its kind published in 1876.

This book is not an extensive study of Baptist history in America. It only tells of the events about our brethren surrounding the War for Independence and highlights the influence they had in the years before, during, and after that great conflict for freedom.

If you are interested in a more detailed, documented look at our rich Christian heritage and how we were established as one nation *"under God"* – consider reading, *America: A Journey of Faith and Freedom.*

The wealth of information within the following pages ought to be known by every independent Baptist today. This book will deepen your appreciation for our denomination's heritage in America, and the influence they had on the founding of our nation. I am proud to be an American. I am proud to be a Bible-believing Christian. But, furthermore, I am proud to be a Baptist!

- Evangelist Caleb Garraway
Founder of Remnant Ministries

A Brief Background

Since the time of Christ, "Baptists" have always been a people whose sole authority was the absolute truth of God's Word. What they believed did not derive from their own philosophical beliefs or from a church's creed, nor was it drawn from surrounding circumstances or religions – it was taken directly from the principles and precepts clearly taught in the Bible.

In your study of general Baptist history, you will find that the first name given to God's people was "Christians", according to Acts 11:26. The next foremost label they received was in A.D. 251 after they broke fellowship with other churches that began to openly accept heretical teachings concerning baptism. They were called "Ana-Baptists."

Ana-Baptists refused to perform baptism on infants and rejected baptism as a means of salvation. They believed what the Bible clearly taught: that a person should only be baptized after they have put their faith and trust in Jesus as their personal Saviour. They believed that baptism signified the first step of obedience for a Christian and his willingness to identify with Christ. They strongly held to the Bible principle of "full immersion" baptism as Christ portrayed and did not agree with "sprinkling" as adopted by the Roman Catholic Church.

Throughout the Dark Ages, depending on the region of Europe they lived in, these Ana-Baptists were also sometimes branded by their critics as Novations, Montanists, Paulicans, or Waldenses. However, they were all the same, and they all severely suffered from the same violent persecution.

Around the beginning of the 16th century, *"Ana-"* was dropped from the name, and they were simply called *"Baptists."* They were not Protestants who came out of the errors of Catholicism during the Reformation as a multitude of other denominations did. Rather, these descendants of the early churches in the book of Acts have always been separate and distinct. *These* are from whom we clearly trace our heritage in world history.

For those who might be unfamiliar with our lineage, I encourage you to read *The Trail of Blood* by

J. M. Carroll and Foxe's *Book of Martyrs* for a spectacular overview of how the Independent Baptist movement came directly from Christ and His disciples.

Since the time of the early church, Bible-believers have been oppressed by every other existing church organization and religion. Every century of our Baptist history has been stained with the blood of brave men and women who unwaveringly stood upon the principles of God's Word. Every effort was made to blot them out from the face of the earth. They were martyred by the hundreds of thousands for their Bible-believing position, robbed of their properties, and driven from country to country.

Nevertheless, their cry for religious liberty and freedom of conscience – not only for themselves and Bible-believing Christianity, but for all mankind – could not be silenced. Finally, in America, though initially mistreated by the state churches of Massachusetts and Virginia (as you will read about), these freedoms were secured for the world to enjoy!

As hard as it is to imagine, Baptists *did* suffer persecution, ridicule, and mockery in the New World. Though it was not widespread, it was still prevalent. This persecution finally subsided when the Declaration of Independence was signed, and then ceased when the Constitution of the United States guaranteed them (and all other denominations) the fullest liberty any people anywhere could possibly experience.

BAPTISTS & THE AMERICAN REVOLUTION

The origin of the Baptists in America is not traceable to any one man or set of men. They did not follow a specific leader; they were simply Bible-believing Christians who genuinely held to the principles and precepts of God's Word. They came to the New World as individuals, families, and small church groups in search of political and religious freedom.

Baptists have never been ones to instigate violence, but they have always been the ardent friends of civil and religious liberty. Their history in America overflows with testimonies of this character. Though they have never regarded fighting, killing, and bloodshed with much favor, they resorted to arms and picked up their weapons in great emergencies to protect their families, their freedoms, and their future when the need arose. Ultimately, they found nothing so dreadful as voluntary slavery to a tyrannical government.

In the Colonies, most Americans were patriots, dynamic for the cause of liberty. But, some were Tories – those who were against the Revolution and remained loyal to the Crown. History records that none of our Baptist ancestors were British sympathizers, with the exception of two or three ministers at the most. That is all! Our Baptists forefathers were patriots!

Baptist pastors (as well as many preachers from other denominations) understood what was at stake in this struggle for freedom. Even a handful of years before the War began, they openly advocated the necessity to break free from the tyranny of Great Britain. In a widely reprinted 1772 sermon from Second Baptist Church in Boston, Pastor John Allen argued on scriptural grounds that the colonists needed to throw off the yoke of the monarchy and declare themselves an independent nation.

Many Baptist pastors and laymen became chaplains or officers in the Continental Army, and their members became soldiers. A countless, unnamed host of our brethren stepped forward without a second's hesitation to face and endure the brutality of war so that we might enjoy the sweet freedoms we have today.

Ministers and members who were not able to fight sent as much aid as they could in support of the war effort. One such example is Christopher Sower, a printer and Baptist preacher in the Philadelphia area. He provided unbound Bibles from his own shop to furnish cartridge paper for the Continental Army during the Battle of Germantown.

For many years, the extensive but out-of-the-spotlight influence Baptists had upon America during the War for Independence has gone unnoticed by many. Inspiring stories and insightful history of our brethren fill the following pages, as we cover the crucial years of 1765-1788, and reveal just how instrumental Independent Baptists really were in the fight for freedom.

John Gano baptizing General George Washington

Setting the Example

Many people from many Christian denominations deserve a fund of glory for their struggles and sacrifices during the American Revolution. Men of nearly every Christian denomination aided in obtaining for our country its greatest possession, and for the world the richest treasure – freedom. All Christian communities in the thirteen Colonies labored with quickened zeal to secure our liberties, and through God's strength, they achieved it.

We will not lessen any amount of glory those of other denominations may want to claim for the Revolutionary War – as long as they allow our Baptist fathers to enjoy the position that their unsurpassed fidelity and heroism justly earned. It is exciting to examine how these men played such an integral role in the establishment of our nation.

But our Baptist ancestors were instrumental even *before* the War for Independence began – in how they responded Biblically to unjust laws, in the establishment and purposes of Rhode Island, and in recognizing Continental Congress as a legitimate legislative body.

A Biblical Response

Just before the Revolution, our ancestors gave the American colonies an impressive example of how to correctly stand up for what was right and how to disobey wicked laws in the right spirit. The Baptists in this country were moral men of character who promoted Christ-honoring living. They would not have perpetrated something that they knew to be wrong for the entire world to see, disgracing our Saviour's name.

Nevertheless, they understood that God had given every man the freedom to worship and to share the Good News of Christ with all people. This was a liberty that no man or government had the right to infringe upon or regulate how it was to be performed. The Baptists did not believe that it was necessary to be "licensed" by a state church to preach (as some states had ordered) or to have written permission to publicly worship God. Nor did they agree with the widespread practice of infant baptism or the belief that baptism was a means for salvation. This caused many to look at our Baptist fathers in a negative and critical way.

Unfortunately, Massachusetts (Congregationalists) and Virginia (Episcopalians), the two leading colonies of the Revolution, were hostile to the Baptists in the years leading up to the War, and had lent their aid to laws that grievously took advantage of them.

By this time, Massachusetts had come under the tight rule of the Massachusetts Bay Colony. Originally, there were two bodies in this state – Massachusetts Bay and Plymouth Colony. Plymouth began with the Pilgrims and the others adventurous enough to come over to the American wilderness in the beginning of the 1600s. The Pilgrims originally never wanted a "state church" to be established; this was the very thing they fled from when they left England and came to the shores of America. They believed in civil liberty and the privilege to freely worship God however one believed, according to the Bible.

But after they chartered a course across the Atlantic and established a colony in Massachusetts, others came – Puritans – who did not see eye to eye with their beliefs. They established Massachusetts Bay. Before long, the Massachusetts Bay Colony in Boston was in control and the Puritan's Congregationalism was established as the "state religion" by law across the entire state.

By the year 1664, the following act was passed, intended to operate directly against Baptists: *"It is ordered and agreed, that if any person or persons, within this jurisdiction, shall either openly condemn or oppose the baptizing of infants, or go about secretly to seduce others from the approbation or use thereof, or shall purposely depart the congregation at the ministration of the ordinance...after due time and means of conviction – every such person or persons shall be sentenced to banishment."*[1]

A certain Brother Painter realized after studying his Bible, that baptism came after salvation – not before – and discovered nothing in God's Word teaching that babies should be baptized. He therefore refused for his child to be baptized according to public law. He was promptly reported to the court system, which with judicial dignity interposed their authority upon his family. As they forced his infant to be immersed, he cried out in rage that infant baptism was an anti-Christian ordinance (which it is); he was then tied up and brutally whipped.

After assembling for years in private dwellings, the First Baptist Church in Boston decided to build a house for their meetings in 1677. Once it was discovered what they were using that house for, it was immediately closed by order of the Massachusetts General Court. After some time they ventured to use it again. When discovered for a second time, the doors and windows were nailed shut and the following warning was posted: *"All persons are to take notice, that by order of the court, the doors of this house are shut up, and that they are prohibited from holding any meeting therein, or to open the doors thereof without license from authority till the general court take further order, as they will answer the contrary at their peril."*[2]

In other instances, the state churches of Massachusetts and Virginia infringed upon the Baptists' religious liberty, even taking away lands and placing unlawful taxes against them. As a result of these oppressive laws, a number of people were hesitant to unite with the Baptists, though they held to the same principles in their hearts, in fear of the court's wrath upon their homes and properties. This ill behavior from the Colony also compelled many British Baptists to stay in England who otherwise would have found a home in America.

Nevertheless, our Baptist ancestors calmly and spiritually stood up against these despotic Colonial laws, and refused to back down. Through their readiness to suffer persecution rather than submitting to unjust demands in conflict with their consciences, the attention of the whole nation was aroused. And by this painful method, the suffering Baptists led their fellow countrymen in how to disregard the tyrannical legislation of the mother country when the time came.

Baptists & the American Revolution

The bold character in the hearts of our Baptist brethren to unashamedly yet gracefully preach the truth of God's Word and not give in to the heresy of infant baptism was fueled by the testimony of Obadiah Holmes, who suffered persecution over a century before in 1651.

Obadiah Holmes was born in Great Britain in 1606 and was raised as a Puritan. He and his wife Catherine fled from England and sailed to America in 1638 in search for religious liberty when King Charles I began to persecute Baptists and other religious groups who did not agree with the doctrinal positions of the Anglican church.

They settled in Salem, Massachusetts, but, unable to bear the civil and religious restrictions that had been established there, they moved to Seekonk in the Massachusetts Bay Colony. As Holmes continued to study the Bible for himself, he saw more and more of the errors in the Puritan church. Finally, he decided to separate from them completely, and he along with a few other families began their own church group.

Now considered to be heretics by those around them, they were threatened by colonial leaders *"to desist, and neither to ordain officers, nor to baptize, nor to break bread together, nor yet to meet upon the first day of the week..."* Not wanting to cause trouble, Obadiah and his wife moved to the newly established Rhode Island, and set up their home for the third and final time. Under the preaching of Pastor John Clarke, Holmes realized that he was a Baptist!

By 1651, those of Obadiah Holmes' family were pillar members of the first Baptist church on American soil, founded and pastored by John Clarke at Newport, Rhode Island. During that summer, William Witter, an aged member of the church and now blind, sent word to Pastor Clarke, asking if someone could come to his home just across the Rhode Island border in Massachusetts and conduct a preaching service for him and some of his neighboring friends.

Upon this request, Pastor John Clarke, layman John Crandall, and preacher Obadiah Holmes immediately started out for Lynn, Massachusetts. After two days' journey, they arrived at Witter's home on Saturday night, July 19, 1651. They enjoyed a time of fellowship and prayer, and spent the evening there, intending to have a service on Sunday. Unknown to these men, the news of their arrival had quickly spread, and soon after, a warrant for their arrest was delivered to the constabulary.

During the Sunday morning worship service, the constables burst into Witter's house and took Clarke, Crandall, and Holmes into custody. They were taken to Boston and on July 31, they were tried in court. Though Clarke presented their defense with a stellar performance, the judge agreed with the prosecution that the "heresy" they preached was worthy of *death*.

But, the court decided to lower the severity of their supposed crimes (preaching against infant baptism and believing as they did) to simply two choices: admit guilt and pay a hefty fine (which none of them could monetarily afford) or refuse admitting guilt and be publicly whipped.

Money was raised by their brethren to pay the fines. Crandall was released. But Clarke and Holmes, knowing what the alternative was, refused for their fines to be paid, not willing to admit guilt. They were left in prison for over a month until September 5, 1651 when they were led to the whipping posts.

As they made their way through the scoffing crowd, someone pressed a large sum of money into the hands of the Puritan official accompanying the group and begged for Clarke to be released. Clarke was a frail older man and the whipping would have probably killed him. Clarke, against his will, was immediately released but was forced to watch his brother in Christ mercilessly whipped.

Holmes was tied to the post and stripped to the waist. As the whip's three cords slammed onto his bare back, Holmes endured it without flinching. According to witnesses, Obadiah did not groan or scream. Instead, he used his suffering as an opportunity to be a testimony for Christ and preach to the crowd, exhorting them to stay faithful to Christ and to not let others bully them from what the Bible clearly teaches.

He also preached of Christ crucified and some accepted the Lord as their Saviour. This infuriated his persecutors who mercilessly and brutally beat him thirty times (the same as that of rapists). The flogger stopped three times to spit on his hands and whipped him with all his might. Many in the gathering crowd cried out in protest. At least thirteen individuals were arrested for calling for the punishment to stop.

When the whipping was over and though he was badly wounded, Holmes said, *"You have struck me as with roses."* He remained in Boston for several weeks while he recovered, only able to eat while kneeling on his elbows and knees.

Holmes gave this account of his beating: *"As the man began to lay the strokes upon my back, I said to the people, though my flesh should fail, yet God will not fail: so it pleased the Lord to come in, and fill my heart and tongue as a vessel full, and with audible voice I break forth, praying the Lord not to lay this sin to their charge, and telling the people I found He did not fail me, and therefore now I should trust Him forever who failed me not: for in truth, as the strokes fell upon me, I had such a spiritual manifestation of God's presence as I never had before and the outward pain was so removed from me, that I could well bear it, yea, and in a manner felt it not, although it was grievous."* Obadiah Holmes considered it an honor to be counted worthy to suffer for Christ and the sake of truth.

BAPTISTS & THE AMERICAN REVOLUTION

In 1652, Holmes succeeded Clarke as pastor of the Newport Baptist Church, the first Baptist church established in America. He led them for almost thirty years, until his death in 1682. Obadiah Holmes' godly testimony stirred our Baptist ancestors to stand up for what is right!

In June 1768, three Baptist ministers – John Waller, Lewis Craig, and James Childs – were arrested in Spottsylvania county, Virginia, on the charge of "preaching the Gospel contrary to law."

"May it please, your worship," said the prosecuting attorney, *"they cannot meet a man on the road without ramming a text of Scripture down his throat."*

For refusing to pledge themselves to stop preaching in that county for a year and a day, these men were thrown into jail with no mention of when they would be released. As they were led through the streets of Fredericksburg to the county prison, they united in singing a hymn well-known in their day:

> *"Broad is the road that leads to death,*
> *And thousands walk together there;*
> *But wisdom shows a narrow path,*
> *With here and there a traveller."*[8]

While in prison, they proclaimed the glorious Gospel through their cell doors and windows to the spiritually hungry throngs who gathered to listen. Infuriated, the local government let them go a few weeks later after seeing their great influence on the people. When they were set at liberty, they went forth resuming their labors with redoubled vigor, gathering fortitude from their late sufferings and thanking God that they were counted worthy to suffer for Christ.[4]

Another time, a handful of Baptist preachers were arrested for supposedly disturbing the peace without a license or permission from the Episcopal Church and were also brought before the magistrates of Spottsylvania County, Virginia, for trial. The crime, as specified in the indictment against these men, was, *"For preaching the Gospel of the Son of God in the colony of Virginia without license."*

It was at this trial that Patrick Henry appeared in their defense, having ridden some 50-60 miles in order to be present. He poured forth such a torrent of burning eloquence that the judge stopped him before he got through with his argument, and said, *"Sheriff, discharge those men!"*

At times, there were those in Virginia who would *"fabricate and spread the most groundless reports, which were injurious to the character of the Baptists. When any Baptist fell into any improper conduct, it was always exaggerated to the utmost extent."*[5]

In the Middlesex and Caroline counties of Virginia, many Baptist ministers were imprisoned for preaching; the jails into which they were cast were loathsome with vermin and filled with disease. They were subjected to the same treatment as criminals and murderers, and no legal efforts were left untried to stifle their earnest efforts in reaching the lost.[6]

William Webber and Joseph Anthony were imprisoned in Chesterfield county for preaching Christ. After they were cast into prison, they began inviting the people through their windows to gather around the walls of the jail at specific meeting times so they could proclaim to them the Good News. They preached through the grates of their cell windows and many professed faith in Christ as a result of their continued efforts.[7] This started a revival among the communities. It was in Chesterfield county that the Baptists flourished, more than any other place in Virginia.

Soon after Webber and Anthony were set free and returned to their homes, Webber joined his fellow preachers John Waller, James Greenwood, Robert Ware, and a layman by the name of Thomas Waford, and continued to travel, preaching the Gospel everywhere they went. As they conducted meetings in the upper part of Middlesex county, they were arrested yet again. Each of these men was taken one by one into private rooms, and the officers attempted to bribe them to not preach in the county again. Each of them expressly refused. Since Waford was not a preacher, he was discharged; but before he was, he was fervently beaten by one of the persecutors with a whip. He carried the scars from this torturous experience to his grave years later.

That night, from the flicker of their candlelight, the men noticed that their prison cell was swarming with fleas. After spending some time singing praises to God and expressing their thanks to Him that it was a prison and not hell that they were in, they prayed for themselves, their friends, their enemies and persecutors, and lay down to sleep. The next morning, many came to hear these men preach. So many people came that their enemies were enraged, and frequently beat on a drum while they were preaching in attempts to distract the people from listening to these men of God.

"The Lord daily opened the hearts of the people; the rich sent many presents, things calculated to nourish them in their sufferings, and to alleviate their sorrows. William Webber fell sick, this excited the sympathy of their friends in a higher degree: they paid him great attention. The persecutors found that the imprisonment of the preachers, tended rather to the furtherance of the Gospel. They preached regularly in prison; crowds attended; the preaching seemed to have double weight when coming from the jail: many viewed it with superstitious reverence, so that their enemies became desirous to be rid of them."[8]

Pastor James Ireland was a young fiery preacher whom God was using in a great way to stir revival in

Virginia. He was thrown into prison time and again, but regardless of this, he kept on preaching. Frequently, he was put in the same cell with drunkards and ruffians, and the godless jailers would encourage his cellmates to beat him up. Nonetheless, Ireland persisted in preaching through his window bars and drew large audiences. Perhaps one of the most disgraceful actions ever taken against him was when two of his burly opponents pulled up a bench and urinated in his face as he tried to preach.

Once, while in jail, an effort was made to kill him by putting gunpowder under the floor of his cell to blow him up, but it was unsuccessful. Then his enemies tried to suffocate him by filling his little room with the stifling fumes of burning brimstone and pepper-pods.[9] Finally, his physician and jailor conspired to poison him by contaminating his food. Though the attempt did not immediately destroy him, he never fully recovered from the effects of the lethal dose of poison he had received.[10]

Brother John Weatherford was cast into prison for *"preaching the gospel of the Son of God."* As he expounded the Scriptures to large crowds from his cell, the magistrates attempted to stop him by building a wall around his prison so he would not be able to see if people had gathered to hear him preach. Nevertheless, when the congregation was assembled, one of his men tied a handkerchief to the end of a pole and raised it high over the top of the barricades, as a signal for him to commence preaching. Souls continued to be saved, lives were touched, and families were strengthened and changed for the glory of God. Weatherford's imprisonment continued for five more months, until someone anonymously paid the hefty fine for his release. He was liberated through the generosity of Patrick Henry.

Baptist ministers were mobbed, beaten, and whipped. Sometimes while they were baptizing converts, men on horseback would ride into the water and try to turn baptism into ridicule. They were often interrupted in their sermons by scoffers and publicly insulted.[11]

From what we can find in court records, as compiled by Lewis Peyton Little in *Imprisoned Preachers and Religious Liberty*, other persecutions to Baptists included being pelted with apples and stones, abducted and nearly drowned by a gang of twenty men, arrested as a vagabond and schismatic, pulled down and hauled about by the hair, having drunken rowdies put in the same prison cell, being dragged off stage and kicked and cuffed about, shot with a shotgun, beaten by ruffians armed with bludgeons, and severely beaten with whips by both people and public officials.

Local authorities would try to break up the crowds by sending horsemen to ride among them, trampling and beating them. Half drunken outcasts were hired to yell out profanities and scream out to drown out their voices.[12] But neither imprisonment, persecution, public disgrace or attempted murder could stop or silence our courageous ancestors – both those who would preach and those who would listen to the preaching. As a result, the Spirit of God tremendously blessed their testimonies and witness.

When they were hunted like wild beasts, and denounced as wolves in sheep's clothing, they meekly replied, *"If we are wolves and our persecutors the true sheep, it is unfathomable that they should treat us with such cruelty. Wolves destroy sheep. It was never known until now that sheep would prey upon wolves."*[13] And they went forth, in violation of the law and in contempt for all illegal opposition, as they continued to "prey" upon the unconverted sheep in order to bring all Virginia to Jesus.

Baptist historian William Fristoe wrote in 1808, *"By a law then in force in Virginia, all* [Baptists] *were under obligation to go to* [the state] *church several times in the year; the failure subjected them to fine. Little notice was taken of the omission, if members of the Established church; but so soon as the* [Baptists] *were absent, they were presented by the grand jury, and fined according to law."*[14]

Dr. Francis Hawks, an Episcopalian, was honest enough to testify, *"No dissenters in Virginia experienced, for a time, harsher treatment than did the Baptists. They were beaten and imprisoned, and cruelty taxed its ingenuity to devise new modes of punishment and annoyance.*"15

Ironically, by 1792 in Virginia, the Baptists had members integrated in every aspect of society, and their congregations had become more numerous than any other Christian denomination!

In New England, Baptists were frequently arrested for not paying taxes to support the state church and clergy.[16] Sometimes, their properties were seized, and generally sold for a mere trifle to pay the church dues not only for themselves but also for their neighbors! Tax collectors in Sturbridge, Massachusetts, *"took pewter from the shelves, skillets, kettles, pots and warming pans, workmen's tools and spinning wheels. They drove away geese and swine and cows, and where there was but one it was not spared. A brother, recently ordained, returned to Sturbridge for his family, when he was thrust into prison, and kept during the cold winter till some one paid his fine and released him. Brother Perry was robbed of a baby's cradle and a steer; Brothers Bloice, Fisk, Streeter, Robbins, Collier, Newel, Smith, Cory, and Barstow were plundered of their household goods and cows, and their liberty for a season."*17

This happened throughout the New England colonies, except in Rhode Island. Our fathers would far rather submit to robbery and loathsome prisons with foul associates rather than render willing obedience to inappropriate and unjust laws. They believed and preached the following from prison windows and pulpits across America, *"Unrighteous laws are conspiracies against God and against the best interests of our race. They are the plots of the Evil One – to be met by exposure and stern resistance. Disobedience to which is loyalty to Jehovah!"* And the multitudes of America heard them. Many did not agree with how the Baptists were being treated.

Once King George III resolved to levy unjust taxations upon the American Colonies without representation, the example of the Baptists became contagious, and resistance to the intolerable tyranny of Great Britain became the occupying thought of the American Colonists.

Many who had oppressed Baptists before the Revolution were grieved as they realized that the very thing now happening to them was what they had subjugated their own brothers unto. God used the fiery trials of the Baptists to enlighten the minds of our forefathers in understanding the importance of standing up for liberty no matter the cost.

As the Baptists engaged in the War, it was not easy to join the same military company with the tax-gatherer who had robbed and swindled them, or with the judge who had condemned them, or with the constable who had thrown them into prison because they refused to support a state religion. It was difficult to stand on the battlefield and fight beside the jailer who had put them in stocks or with the persecutor who scourged them and mistreated them for preaching Jesus.

Nevertheless, our brethren put their feelings aside and vitally aided in the securing of our liberties. Our Baptist fathers forgave their oppressors; and, in view of the great dangers threatening all that they held dear, they stood shoulder to shoulder with these fellow patriots. They never gave up the conflict until the flag of freedom floated in undisturbed majesty over the entire territory claimed by the thirteen Colonies.

RHODE ISLAND
"The Safe Haven"

Roger Williams was an independent Baptist preacher and missionary to the Indians who advocated the freedom of religion and true political liberty. He publically protested against the *"Law of Patents"* (a policy originally established by the popes in Rome during the Middle Ages) that authorized "Christian" kings and governments to claim land inhabited by conquest or discovery. The Puritans used this to justify their confiscation of land that rightfully belonged to the

Native Americans. To Roger Williams, this was nothing but robbery.

He also strongly opposed the *"Enforcement of the First Table of the Law"* (instituted by the Puritans), which gave national government the right to impose religious beliefs upon their citizens.

He founded Rhode Island in 1636, after he and his family were banished from the Massachusetts Bay Colony as a result of his strong preaching. When Williams and several of his friends settled in the territory that would soon be Rhode Island, they *bought* their land from the Native Americans. While other colonies were established on land seized from the Native Americans, Williams remained true to his beliefs. The Massachusetts Bay leadership laughed at Williams and his friends for wasting so much money as they did on Rhode Island, for they considered that land to be the "sewer of New England."

Williams was burdened of God to begin a colony that would exhibit true religious and political liberty without bias. After they were incorporated as a state in 1644, they passed the following law: *"Every man who submits peaceably to civil government in this colony shall worship God according to the dictates of his own conscience without molestation. All men may walk as their own consciences persuade them, every one in the name of his God."*[18]

From that point, Rhode Island became a safe harbor for any person seeking religious asylum. Catholics, Muslims, Jews, Atheists, and Baptists (among others) lived peaceably together in this colony! When the United States Constitution was adopted, *"Rhode Island,"* says her historian, Arnold, *"for more than a century and a half had enjoyed a freedom unknown to any of her peers, ...civil and religious freedoms which are now everywhere received in America."*[19]

John Leland summarized this Baptist spirit: *"Let every man speak freely without fear, maintain the principles that he believes, worship according to his own faith, either one God, three gods, no god, or twenty gods; and let government protect him in doing so."*[20] (This has always been the spirit of true Bible-based Baptists. The problem in today's generation is that atheists and other liberal groups want to enjoy this freedom, but they do not want to reciprocate religious tolerance or acceptance to Bible-believing Christianity.)

Rhode Island ultimately became a haven for the independent Baptists. Morgan Edwards, a man of great historical learning, who died in 1795, wrote: *"The Baptists have always been more numerous than any other sect of Christians in Rhode Island; two-fifths of the inhabitants, at least are reputed Baptists. The governors, deputy-governors, judges, assembly-men and officers, civil and military, are chiefly of that persuasion."*[21]

Besides this demonstration of true liberty, Rhode Island and its founding documents blazed the trail for the establishment of the American republic. It and the influence of the Independent Baptists played a key role in the philosophies and principles behind the American government that our Founding Fathers established.

The *"Providence Compact,"* penned in Providence, Rhode Island, was the first document in America that gave power to the government only from and by the consent of the governed. It also instituted the principle *"liberty of conscience."* It was visionary for its time!

The *"Portsmouth Compact,"* rarely given the credit it deserves, was uniquely powerful because of its guarantee of religious liberty, and was the first government document that indirectly severed both political and religious ties with England. Over twenty men signed their names to this Christian parchment: *"We whose names are underwritten, do here solemnly, in the presence of Jehovah, incorporate ourselves into a body politic, and as He shall help, will submit our persons, lives and estates, unto our Lord Jesus Christ, the King of kings, and Lord of lords, and to all those perfect and most absolute laws of His, given us in His holy Word of truth, to be guided and judged thereby."*

The *"Rhode Island Constitution,"* written by Dr. John Clarke, pastor of the first Baptist Church in

America, is believed by many to be the very basis of the United States Constitution.

Rhode Island, as early as 1764, foresaw the coming Revolutionary storm and helped our Founding Fathers establish the *"Committee of Correspondence"* system. Its special duty was to stir up the American people in maintaining their God-given liberties and to orchestrate cooperation among the thirteen Colonies.[22] This movement directly assisted in bringing about the First Continental Congress.

Before the Revolution, Rhode Island was the freest Colony in North America and in the history of our nation. Her Baptist founders had made their settlement a Republic complete in every aspect of liberty, even while under the nominal rule of the British Crown. Rhode Island did not have a viceroy *(an official who runs a colony or province in the name of and as representative of the monarch)*. The king did not have the power to veto any of her laws. They created a government with which there could be no lawful interference by any European power or by any of the fellow colonies on American soil.

In March 1663, it was enacted that *"no tax should be imposed or required of the Colony but by the act of the General Assembly."*[23] In 1704, Mompesson, the chief-justice of New York, wrote Lord Nottingham that *"when he was in Rhode Island, the people acted in all things as if they were outside the dominion of the crown."*[24] Bancroft spoke of Rhode Island that they were *"enjoying a form of government, under its charter, so thoroughly republican that no change was required beyond a renunciation of the king's name in the style of its public acts"*[25] when it became a state of the Union.

On May 4, 1776, just two months before the adoption of the Declaration of Independence, Rhode Island rejected every form of allegiance to King George III.[26] This little State withdrew itself from the control of the British Empire thirty-two days[27] before the brave and patriotic Virginians had renounced allegiance to the English king and while the other Colonies were still hesitant.

Rhode Island joined early in the struggle for freedom and fought hard until victory rested upon all of America. Scarcely had the retreating troops of General Gage reached Boston from Lexington and Concord when the nearest of Rhode Island towns sent reinforcements to their Massachusetts brethren in arms. The Rhode Island legislature soon after voted that 1,500 more men should be sent to the frontlines.

When the Declaration of Independence was read aloud in Newport, East Greenwich, and Providence, Rhode Island, people enthusiastically celebrated and rejoiced that true *"liberty o'er and o'er the globe"*[28] was finally announced. Finally, a nation with ultimate freedoms had been born into the world!

The people of Newport, Rhode Island, courageously removed forty pieces of artillery from the British fort to a secure location, where the cannons might be ready for the defense of their homes, instead of them being used by the British for the destruction of Boston and other densely populated key cities.

A British historian wrote: *"The Rhode Islanders were such ardent patriots that after the capture of the island of Rhode Island by Sir Peter Parker, it required a great body of men to be kept there, in perfect idleness, for three years, to retain them in subjection."*[29]

In 1781 Governor William Green, in a letter to George Washington said, *"Sometimes every fencible man in the State, sometimes a third, and at other times a fourth part, was called out upon for duty."*[30] Rhode Island *never* halted for a moment in her courageous efforts.

With less than 50,000 citizens, this Baptist-born state supported three full regiments in the Continental Army throughout the *entire* war, besides the men they employed for their local defenses during the Revolution.[31]

Rhode Island – this safe harbor of personal and religious freedom – was a prime example to the rest of the Colonies of patriotism. Rhode Island also demonstrated a wonderful testimony of how precious unhindered liberty is for all people to enjoy.

Recognizing the Authority of Continental Congress

Independent Baptists were the first denomination in America to recognize the Continental Congress as a legitimate government and legislative body.

On September 5, 1774, in Independence Hall, the first Continental Congress assembled and deliberated about the plight of the United States' colonies. The eyes of the entire American people rested upon it, and so did the hearts and hopes of a vast majority of our Baptist ancestors. Eight days after Congress first met, the Warren Association of Baptist Churches (who represented the Baptist churches of New England) solemnly recognized it as, in a sense, the Supreme Court of the American colonies. They also sent it this appeal:

"*HONORED GENTLEMEN: As the Baptist Churches in New England are most heartily concerned for the preservation and defense of the rights and privileges of this country, and are deeply affected by the encroachments upon the same which have been lately made by the British Parliament, and are willing to unite with our dear countrymen to pursue every prudent measure for relief, so, we would beg leave to say, that as a distinct denomination, we conceive that we have an equal claim to charter rights with the rest of our fellow-subjects, and yet we have been long denied the free and* full enjoyment of those rights, as to the support of religious worship..."⁸² Then they wrote a full appeal for such relief as Congress, by legitimate means, was able to secure to their brethren who were suffering from religious persecution.

The Philadelphia Baptist Association, the oldest body of this character in America, sent a large committee to Congress to aid in the appeal of what their New England brethren had written and requested. Dr. Samuel Jones, in his sermon before the Philadelphia Association at its meeting in 1807, said: *"On the assembling of the first Continental Congress, I was one of the committee, under appointment of your body, that, in company with the late Reverend Isaac Backus of Massachusetts, met the delegates in Congress, to see if we could not obtain some security for that liberty for which we were then fighting and bleeding at their side. It seemed unreasonable to us that we should be called to stand up with them in defense of liberty, if, after all, it was to be a liberty for one party to oppress another."*⁸³

These two Baptist bodies formally recognized the Revolution and the Continental Congress, but they did not publicly stand with Congress only to gain something from them; they believed that the Congress's patriotic position was Biblically correct. Nevertheless, the Baptists found nothing wrong in seeking much needed relief on the behalf of their brethren facing persecution.

Of course, the Baptists would have never associated with our Founding Fathers or formally recognized them in the first place if they believed that their cause was unjust or their actions unholy. The conscientious Baptist – who unashamedly preached Bible principles (though imprisoned and scourged for it), who refused to pay taxes to support the State clergy (though certain to be thrust into jail for his disobedience), and whose properties were seized and sold for less than half of their worth by the officers of the law – would have borne the worst of penalties ever endured rather than recognize a legislative body tainted with usurpation and evil rebellion. Our Baptist ancestors would have borne any atrocity before they would have accepted relief by or from an unholy means.

On December 9, 1774, the Continental Congress (at the time simply a provincial government with no real power as of yet – simply men deliberating what their actions would be in response to the tyranny from the British crown) made the following reply to the petition of the Baptists:

"Resolved, that the establishment of civil and religious liberty, to each denomination in the province, is the sincere wish of this Congress. But being by no means vested with powers of civil government, whereby they can redress the grievances of any person whatsoever, they therefore recommend to the Baptist churches, that when a General Assembly shall be

convened in their colony, they lay the real grievances of said churches before the same, when and where their petition will most certainly meet with all that attention due to the memorial of a denomination of Christians so well disposed to the public weal of their country." – Signed by John Hancock and Benjamin Franklin.

Though the Baptists did not initially receive freedom from their persecutors, this letter was a great consolation to know that our Founding Fathers were in agreement with them. And, as the Constitution was being penned and there was possibility for the guarantee of religious liberties, our Baptist forefathers did all in their power to see something amended by our government to secure these rights.

In seeking relief from the Continental Congress, the two most influential Baptist organizations in the land gave that Assembly their formal approval. These endorsements, publicly bestowed at a time when doubt and alarm prevailed everywhere, had *a powerful influence* in confirming the faith of our fathers and helped established the righteous character of their deliberations.

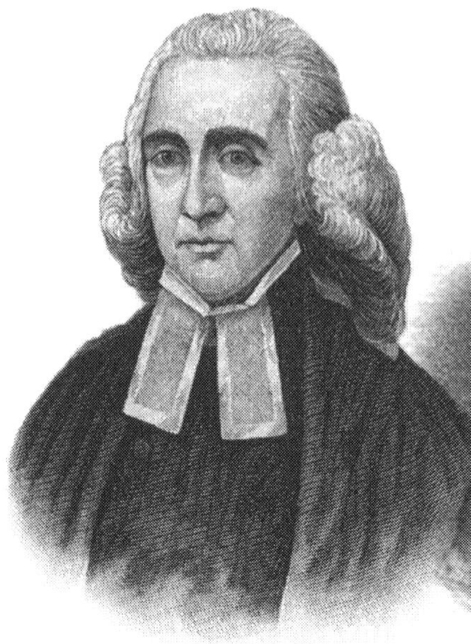

Samuel Stillman

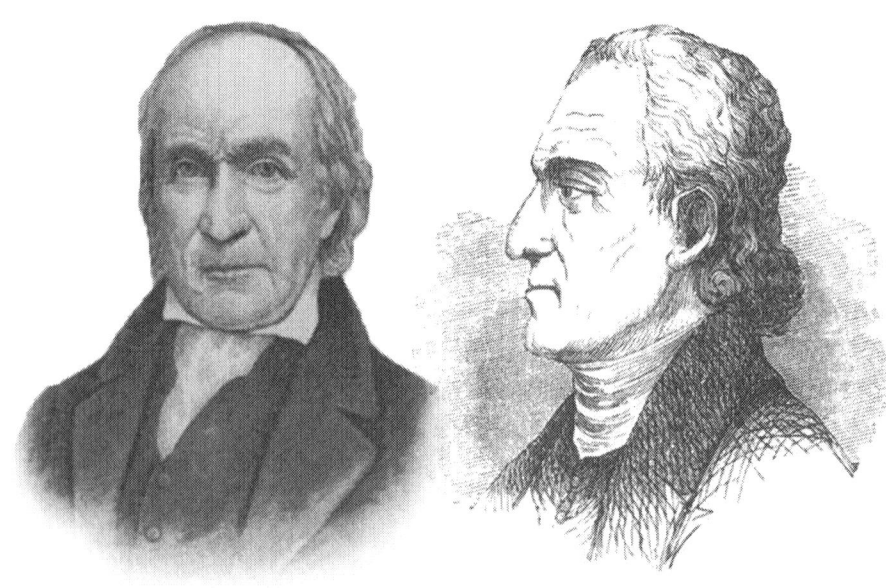

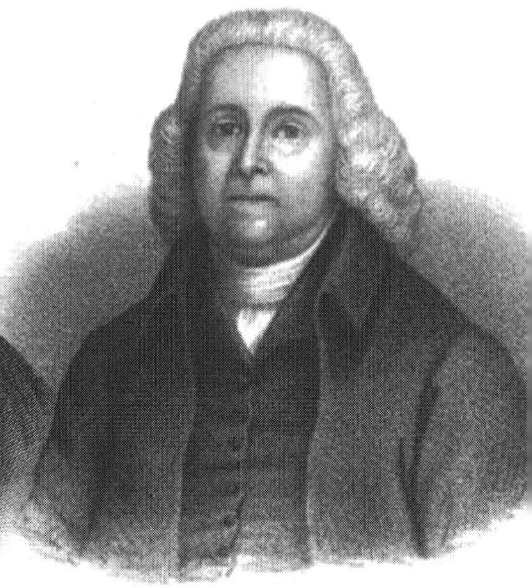

Isaac Backus

John Leland

David Jones

Notable Baptist Preachers during the American Revolution

Advocates of Liberty

Baptists have always been the supporters and promoters of political and religious liberty. They believed that God had created men equally given them certain rights that no government could strip away – life, liberty, and the pursuit of happiness.

They also always have claimed the right for themselves, and for others, to worship God according to their understanding of His Word. They have always stood against the union of a State with a church, and have refused to accept any legislation in favor of religious matters for themselves and opposed it for others. Their desire has been for men to have the chance to freely worship God according to their beliefs.

Therefore, their aid in securing liberty was of the highest importance.

The Baptist General Association of Virginia notified the Convention of the general spirit among the entirety of the people in that state (which was a steadily growing number of Baptists). They wrote, *"They had considered what part it would be proper to take in the unhappy contest, and had determined that they ought to make a military resistance to Great Britain in her unjust invasion, tyrannical oppression, and repeated hostilities."*[84] And they proclaimed to the world that *"they were in favor of the Revolution."*[85] This action undoubtedly held some weight with the Convention, whose delegates voted for the Declaration of Independence the next year in the Continental Congress.

Preachers and their people were captivated with thoughts and ways of how to aid and successfully affect the War for Independence in favor of the Colonies. This ardent patriotism not only caused them to send supplies when they could to help meet the needs of the troops, and to volunteer as soldiers in the Continental Army, but it also led many ministers to leave their pulpits in the capable hands of laymen-preachers and become chaplains in the Continental Army.

Having unbounded confidence in the power of prayer, they were eager to be with our armed heroes in the camps, hospitals, and battlefields. They were holy men of God who unflinchingly stood in harm's way so that they might point their brothers to the Saviour in the hardest of sufferings and pray while fighting on the battlefield to the Lord of Hosts for success and protection in every deadly conflict that they faced.

In this spirit, Baptist ministers were more than willing to join the army as chaplains. Leading pastors from every state were with Washington and his troops in each difficulty, deprivation, and peril of the Revolutionary War.

CHAPLAINS IN THE ARMY

In 1775, the Baptist General Association of Virginia (which represented a large portion of our denomination at that time in the southern states) applied to the convention of their State for permission to preach among the Army regiments encamped in their area. Their request was granted, and the Association sent Brother Jeremiah Walker and Brother John Williams to address the soldiers. These two men were among some of the most popular Baptist preachers of their day among the troops.[36]

Pastor M'Clanahan raised a company of soldiers in Culpeper County to join the Continental Army, led them into battle as their captain, and ministered unto them as a chaplain.[37]

Pastor Charles Thompson of Massachusetts was a Bible scholar, an eloquent preacher, and a man of genuine godliness whose dynamic and excited personality vibrantly boosted our patriots' morale. He gave three years of his life in harms' way serving as a chaplain in the Army before the British captured him. The enemy considered him such a threat that they burned down his church, his parsonage, and several other private dwellings in his community to force him to return home. He refused, and as a result, they caught him, carried him away prisoner, and kept him on board a guard ship.[38]

Dr. Hezekiah Smith tenderly pastored his church in Haverhill, Massachusetts. He was a reserved man of refined and dignified habits, and seemingly was the last minister in his state likely to seek a position in the Continental Army. But, at the outbreak of war, his patriotic ardor was so intense that it tore him from his comfortable, quaint home and stirred him to become a chaplain. It was a great sacrifice for him to leave his flock, because it also meant for him to leave behind his wife, and his grown children with their families.

In his new position, he discharged the duties of his office with marked fidelity; and, by his cultured manners, wisdom, and bravery in battle, he obtained the confidence of the most distinguished officers in the Army. He became a very close and personal friend of George Washington, who treated him with extraordinary kindness and favor. He served in the Army for five years – boldly preaching against sin and temptations, and warmly encouraging all to confidently put their faith and trust in the Great Captain of our salvation.

Smith was a man filled with the power of God, whose distinguished character provided a great testimony to the troops whom he followed into battle. He had a commanding personality, yet the air of a perfect gentleman. One day, the constable of a neighboring town, to which Dr. Smith had gone to preach, was "a weak and inferior-looking person," but he was full of arrogance. And, armed with the authority of the law, he came *"to warn this stranger – this Baptist – out of the place."* But when he saw the imposing appearance of this man of God, he was confused and stammered out: *"I warn you – off God's earth."*

Smith looked at him humbly, yet amused, and responded, *"My good sir, where shall I go to?"*

"Go anywhere," was the reply; *"Go to the Isle of Shoals."*[89] (The "Isles of Shoals" are a group of small islands and tidal ledges situated approximately six miles off the east coast of the United States, straddling the border of New Hampshire and Maine.[40]) But Hezekiah Smith did not leave God's earth, or visit the Isle of Shoals at that time. He preached the Gospel to the town

where God had sent him and experienced great spiritual success!

Dr. William Rogers, who pastored in Philadelphia, was well-liked and known as a talented preacher. For some time he was the Professor of Oratory at the University of Pennsylvania. Many people frequently read his books and printed sermons. Dr. Benjamin Rush (signer of the Declaration of Independence and Constitution, and influential Founding Father) was a member of his congregation. Many other persons of culture considered him their pastor, waited upon his ministry, and trusted in his godly advice.

He, too, was a personal friend of George Washington. One gentleman who was visiting Rogers, wrote of his experience with Rogers and the visit they made to Washington's residence in Philadelphia: *"Dr. Rogers is a most entertaining and agreeable man, and we were introduced by him to General Washington. When we called, the General was not at home [at the time], but while we were talking with his private secretary in the hall, he came in, and spoke to Dr. Rogers with the greatest ease and familiarity. He immediately asked us up to the drawing-room where Lady Washington and his two nieces were."*[41] There, they proceeded to have a time of food and enjoyable fellowship.

When Pennsylvania raised three battalions of troops for the War, the Legislature appointed Dr. Rogers as their chaplain. He was afterwards promoted as a brigade-chaplain in the Continental Army. For five years, this distinguished man of God followed these brave men into battle. He remained unwearied through the turmoil of war, served as an encouragement, and was beloved by all the troops in his spiritual care.

Pastor David Jones was an educated man with a powerful intellect. He was an original thinker and was fearless in expressing his sentiments. As a preacher, he always captured the undivided attention of his hearers. He never failed in instructing them in the ways of righteousness and cheering them with the Divine Peace that God so frequently gives throughout His Word.

When the Revolutionary War began, Brother Jones lived in a section of New Jersey where Tories made it neither agreeable nor safe for a patriot to reside, especially if – like Jones – he was a brave orator capable of moving men by his eloquence. So Brother Jones, believing that he could serve his country better than by martyrdom, moved to Pennsylvania.

In 1775, during a public fast, he preached to the regiment of Colonel Dewees a sermon overflowing with patriotism, and with unshaken confidence in God. The message was so powerful that it was printed and widely circulated throughout the Colonies. God used it to exert an extensive influence across early America in favor of the "good cause."

In 1776, Brother Jones started out as a chaplain for a Pennsylvania regiment. He preached about independence and repentance among the troops, and he always encouraged their hearts. But, he also was a fierce fighter on the battlefield. He was never away from scenes of danger; nor from the bedside of the sick or the wounded soldier where words of comfort were needed. He followed General Gates through two campaigns, and served as a brigade chaplain under General "Mad" Anthony Wayne.

At the battle of Brandywine, as he rode in the midst of the fighting, his horse was shot out from under him. Jumping to his feet after he had been thrown off his animal, he continued to shoot at the enemy. When his ammunition would not fire, with sheer valor and courage, he flung his pistol in the face of the nearest of the advancing troops and continued to fight. He miraculously survived without injury and continued serving at Valley Forge with Washington until the end of the war when Cornwallis surrendered at Yorktown.

British General Howe, learning that Jones was a pillar to the Revolution in and out of the Army, offered a reward for his capture. And, by the special care of Providence, plots were unsuccessful in capturing him. Full of wit, eloquence, patriotism, and fearless courage, he was a model chaplain, and a tower of strength for the cause of freedom.

John Gano pastored the First Baptist Church in New York City, where – unknown to him – Washington would sit outside the open window of the Baptist church in his carriage and listen to this young man's fervent, heart-filled preaching. Impressed with Gano's passion and testimony, Washington chose him as his personal chaplain. Brother Gano baptized General Washington at Valley Forge in the presence of 42 witnesses around 1780.

The officers and men with whom John Gano often worked considered his help to be necessary and invaluable. He was known to have the testimony of a true Christian. Many testified that his entire conduct was completely controlled by the Spirit of God and that he genuinely walked with God. Furthermore, his genial manners and fearless courage made him the special friend of men and officers of all ranks.

During the battle of Chatterton's Hill, his position was suddenly put under fire from the enemy. *"His cool and quiet courage in thus fearlessly exposing himself was afterwards commented on in the most glowing terms by the officers who stood near him."*[42] Gano wrote of the experience and explained, *"My station in time of action I knew to be among the surgeons, but in this battle I somehow got in front of the regiment; yet I durst not quit my place for fear of dampening the spirits of the soldiers, or of bringing on myself an imputation of cowardice."*[43]

Often, Gano would be found working among the wounded on the battle field to assure them of their eternal destin, but many times he would also be found on the front lines sharing the soldiers' perils and eagerly pushing forward with them. During one instance, when this courageous man of God *"saw more than half the army flying from the sound of cannon, others abandoning their pieces without firing a shot, and a brave band of only six hundred maintaining a conflict with the whole British Army, filled with chivalrous and patriotic sympathy for the valiant men that refused to run, he could not resist the strong desire to share their perils, and he eagerly pushed forward to the front."*[44] Because of this, Gano became known as "the Fighting Chaplain." At the end of the War for Independence, George Washington presented unto Gano the beloved sword that Marquis de Lafayette had given him. This was a symbol of friendship, deep gratitude, and honor for the service Gano had wrought for his country.

He preserved his moral dignity as a Christian minister time and again under the most trying of circumstances and was a stellar testimony of true patriotism. By his Christ-like example, his positive spirit, and his stirring Bible preaching, he assisted the brave soldiers of the Continental Army to endure hardships, to struggle successfully against despair, and

1765-1788

to fight with the courage of men who were sure that God was with them, and that ultimate triumph was certain.

When the War for Independence was finally over and the British flag was being lowered at Yorktown with Old Glory rising on the flagpole to take its place, Washington turned to John Gano and asked him to give the final prayer of praise and thanksgiving unto God for Him granting them the victory.

Men of God stood shoulder-to-shoulder with our Founding Fathers, involved in politics and the ratification of our Constitution and courageously fighting with them on the field of battle. Without question, the preaching, leadership, wisdom, and testimony of God's men were hailed throughout the colonies as the spark that ignited victory and patriotism.

"All these, and a hundred other great and good men, by their example and eloquence fed the fires of liberty, and sustained the courage of the people. Men of learning and culture, they were looked up to for advice and counsel – whose praise was not only in all the churches, but throughout the land, for their integrity, ability, and patriotism.

"These formed a host of devoted laborers in the common cause, but more than this, their prayers rose incessantly, from camp and field, that God would defend the right, and save His people. These last are counted as nothing by the historian, but we may rest

assured that they did more than resolutions of Congress, and acts of committees of safety, towards achieving our liberties.

"One may consider it beneath the dignity of history to put them among the causes that led ultimately to our success: but when that history comes to be read in the light of eternity, the enthusiasm of volunteers and the steady courage of the disciplined battalions will sink into insignificance beside the devoted prayers and faith of these men of God."[45]

We have reason to thank God for these preaching and praying heroes who followed the American flag wherever it went: through hunger, cold winters, discouragements, retreats, diseases, wounds, danger, bloodshed, and finally – victory. These men of God helped keep the eyes of the Continental Army on the Captain of Heaven; and their prayers, combined with those who fought, brought success upon our just cause.

All of those who were engaged in this struggle for freedom clearly saw time and again that the hand of God was thoroughly involved in the War. When General George Washington wrote his farewell orders to the Continental Army on November 2, 1783, he acknowledged, *"The singular interpositions of Providence in our feeble condition were such, as could scarcely escape the attention of the most unobserving; while the unparalleled perseverance of the Armies of the U States, through almost every possible suffering and discouragement for the space of eight long years, was little short of a standing miracle."*

When Washington became our first President under the new Constitution of the United States, he said in his Inaugural Address: *"No people can be bound to acknowledge and adore the Invisible Hand which conducts the affairs of men more than the people of the United States. Every step by which they have advanced to the character of an independent nation seems to have been distinguished by some token of providential agency."*

Elias Boudinot, a delegate of the Continental Congress from New Jersey (who later became a U.S. Congressman and then was appointed by President Washington as Director of the United States Mint), wrote in a letter on August 20, 1783, *"I have been in the midst of the principal scenes of action during the whole contest. I have not been a bare spectator. I have carefully watched and compared the steps of Divine Providence thro' the whole, and as the result I can assure you that our success has not been of the effect of our numbers, power, wisdom, or art. It has been manifestly the effect of the astonishing interposition of a holy God in our favor."*

During the Constitutional Convention, aged Benjamin Franklin testified in his pivotal speech to the delegates, *"In the beginning of the contest with Great Britain, when we were sensible of danger, we had daily prayer in this room for Divine protection. Our prayers were heard, and they were graciously answered. All of us engaged in the struggle must have observed frequent instances of Superintending Providence in our favor."*

This was made possible, in part, because of Bible-believing men of God who helped keep the eyes of the Continental Army upon the Lord and who filled the ranks of the Army with a steadfast faith and hope in Almighty God.

When we read of the self-sacrifice of Baptist preachers like these, it should be no surprise that General George Washington proudly wrote that Independent Baptist chaplains were *"the most prominent and useful in the Army."*[46]

And even the enemy, British General Howe, was constrained to acknowledge that *"the Baptists were among the most strenuous supporters of liberty."*[47]

OTHER PATRIOTIC PREACHERS

Though several Baptist pastors were not able serve as chaplains in the Continental Army, they did strategically aid the American Revolution in other ways essential to the cause of liberty. One of these men was Dr. James Manning, president of the college now known as Brown University. Manning was quite vocal about his support for the War and religious freedom.

Few men in his day (in his own or other denominations) wielded a more extensive influence than he did. His polished manners, his educated mind, his quick perception, his untiring activity, his habit of putting his whole soul into the toils which occupied his time, and the modest ease with which he moved in every aspect of his society, made him a dynamic leader wherever he went.

He never sought the attention of the public eye nor did he ever want a position in government. Nevertheless, the people frequently wanted to hear his opinions. Once, he accidentally entered into the State Legislature while it was in session; and, the members of the Congress unanimously elected him to temporarily fill one of their vacant seats and give them Biblical and prudent counsel on their proceedings.[48]

During the Revolution, he was the most influential man of Rhode Island and was instrumental in the state's survival. With most of the state's men taken away from cultivating their farms to fight in the War, and the enemy occupying a large section of the state, provisions for the remaining citizens, women, and children quickly became scarce.

To make matters worse, at that time, several of the neighboring states had laws forbidding the transportation of food beyond their own limits. This meant that a means of finding a substantial supply for the desperate needs of the people of Rhode Island was a serious problem. Pastor Manning was commissioned by the Governor and the Council of War to somehow obtain relief and aid. Manning zealously attended to this responsibility placed upon him, found a way to make an appeal to the government of Connecticut, and was successful beyond all expectations.[49]

In 1780, Manning allowed his university's campus to become an encampment site for the French soldiers sent by King Louis XVI to aid the Patriots. Additionally, Manning allowed University Hall to be used as a military hospital.

By persons in all positions in life from George Washington down, Pastor James Manning was regarded as one of the influential spiritual leaders during the War for Independence.

Pastor Isaac Backus played a key role in the establishment of religious freedom in our country. He intensely debated this with our Founding Fathers on the political front lines in Independence Hall and Continental Congress. We cannot be thankful enough for the influence of Isaac Backus among Baptists and upon our nation.

Considered a leading orator of the "pulpit of the American Revolution," Backus published several sermons that were widely read and distributed among the New England colonies. Newspapers back then were more of a "novelty" than a consistent source of news and political views. Therefore, the pulpit was the most direct and effective way to reach the people. Up and down the colonies, pastors would often print their political sermons and pass out their pamphlets on Sundays when their churches were flocked with people. These messages quickly spread across their counties and *"became the text books of human rights in every parish."*[50]

Backus' sermon, *An Appeal to the Public for Religious Liberty, Against the Oppressions of the Present Day*, in 1773 boldly announced the need for religious liberty and the abolition of established state churches. Backus declared: *"Now who can hear Christ declare, that his kingdom is, not of this world, and yet believe that this blending of church and state together can be pleasing to him?"* He advocated obedience to government, but also argued that the government had no right to intrude on spiritual authority. He understood that those who blended church and state together usually violated Christ's commands to both.

In 1778, he authored a historically important work entitled *Government and Liberty Described and Ecclesiastical Tyranny Exposed*. Backus also served as a delegate to the Massachusetts Ratifying Convention, which ratified the United States Constitution in 1788. He voted in favor of ratification. We owe our religious liberty to the tireless efforts of this great man of God!

Pastor David Barrow of Virginia exhorted his countrymen to shake off the yoke of British bondage and boldly face the enemy. When dangers pressed, Barrow voluntarily shouldered his musket, joined the army, and was always found ready to go to the frontlines. He became known as a man of notable character on the battlefield with an enthusiastic reputation to never quit.

Brother David was also adamant against the ownership of slaves. His Bible-based opinion was that slavery was a vile sin before God (and it is), and he was of the same mindset as what President Thomas Jefferson wrote, *"God who gave us life gave us liberty. Can the liberties of a nation be secure when we have removed a conviction that these liberties are the gift of God? Indeed I tremble for my country when I reflect that God is just, that his justice cannot sleep forever. Commerce between master and slave is despotism. Nothing is more certainly written in the book of fate than that these people are to be free."*[51]

In fact, Brother David's passionate preaching against slavery caused many to disapprove of him. Nevertheless, he never altered his message throughout the years, and he became a leader of "the Anti-Slavery Baptists." These churches openly accepted slaves in their services and encouraged them to join their membership. They understood that God created ALL men equal, regardless of skin color![52] They believed that in the Bible, there was no white church, black church, brown church, red church, or yellow church – there was only the *blood-bought church* of Jesus Christ. Our Lord did not come to save or prefer a certain skin color, but He came to save souls!

Pastor Daniel Marshall was so strongly identified with the cause of his struggling countrymen that the British arrested him for supposedly "unruly" behavior. They kept him under guard until he realized that God had given him this wonderful opportunity to preach to the British soldiers in the camp where he was imprisoned and to pray in the presence of the officers for the needs of the men. Wanting no part with it, they set him at liberty as soon as he began.[53]

Pastors Oliver Hart, William Drayton and William Tennant were appointed by South Carolina's Council of Safety to travel throughout the state and publicly expound upon the importance of patriotism to the people and what the thirteen Colonies had been fighting for.[54]

Pastor Richard Furman was one of the most active patriot pastors in the South. He surrendered to the call to preach at the age of 16 in 1771 and was ordained as the pastor of High Hills Baptist Church in South Carolina only two years later. During the War for Independence, he volunteered to serve in the Army, but was persuaded that his talents could be better used as a motivational speaker in the South to gain support for the cause and to stir up the hearts of men to enlist. He was so successful and used of God that, when the

British took over Charleston in 1780, General Charles Cornwallis placed a bounty on Furman's head of one thousand English pounds (equivalent to $250,000 in modern American currency). This reward was to be given to the person who could bring him in dead or alive! He was never caught, but continued to frustrate the plans of the enemy until the end of the War.

In recognition of his sacrificial services, he was elected a member of the convention that framed the Constitution of South Carolina.[55]

Pastor Samuel Stillman of Boston was a soft-spoken yet cordial-sounding man who weighed only 97 pounds, with little interest in the affairs of government before the Revolution. Many thought that he would be one of the least involved pastors in the war effort when the time came. But when the rumors of battle began to spread across the Northeast, he became one of the main pastors who enlisted men everywhere. He was involved with his whole heart: no one in Massachusetts was recognized as a more ardent friend of liberty than the pastor of the First Baptist Church of Boston.[56]

He began to preach with such a patriotic fervor that he became one of the most popular preachers during the Revolutionary War. So many people flocked to hear him that they had to build a new facility.

John Adams and Henry Knox frequented his services. John Hancock became one of his church members and was one of his greatest admirers. He rented a pew each week to guarantee seating and so that he could bring his friends and have them listen to Stillman's stirring sermons.

In eloquent terms he advocated the doctrines of independence and continued to unashamedly preach even when the British occupied the city of Boston. After the War, Stillman remained very politically involved, becoming a member of the Senate Convention for the formation of the state's constitution in 1779.

He was also one of the twelve delegates from Boston in the Constitutional Convention. He was used of God in delivering a key speech in the Constitution's support, *"and was considered at the time as having contributed much toward its adoption, and confirmed many members in its favor who were previously wavering upon that question."*[57]

Patriotic Baptist Laymen

Though many Baptist preachers were very influential in the fight for liberty, our faithful laymen brethren who filled the pews across America and filled the ranks of the Continental Army were the most important in this great struggle. A countless number of men put their lives on the line day after day, time and again, suffering through the reality and brutality of war. Yet they fervently pressed on, believing that their faith, families, and freedoms were the most precious and sacred things worth defending. Furthermore, they were willing to shed their blood on the battlefield, if the need arose, to guarantee the survival of what they held dear.

One layman who great contributed to the Revolutionary War was Brother John Hart. He was universally regarded by his peers as one of the best men in New Jersey during his lifetime. He was held in such high esteem that his community often selected him to settle disputes. His neighbors spoke of him affectionately as *"Honest John Hart."* His private and public testimony was genuinely the same – a man of great modesty and benevolence with his highest ambitions being that to serve God and to promote the best interests of his countrymen.

In 1776, he became one of the signers of the Declaration of Independence. He was humbled with this great opportunity to represent his state in Continental Congress and help craft our nation's birth certificate. Two days before this precious document was to be ratified, he received word that the British had landed a part of its powerful army just miles up the road from his farm, gristmill, and home.[58]

As he willingly stepped up and unhesitantly signed his name to the Declaration, he *knew* within his heart that his actions would bring down the vengeance of the British upon his home within a short time. He realized that everything he owned – except the soil upon which his residence stood – would be destroyed. His own life would be taken if he was captured, and he had no idea what would happen to his family.

After the Convention, he hastily returned home to tend to the well being of his family, only to discover that his wife lay dying with sickness and his fields and gristmill were in grave danger of being laid to waste.

Learning that he was back, the British raided his properties a second time to flush him out and capture him. He was driven from the bedside of his dying wife, who courageously encouraged him to flee for the sake of his country. He also ordered his servants and all thirteen of his children to escape into the woods before the British surrounded them and it was too late for them all.

For more than a year he lived in the forests and caves, on the run to evade incarceration and public execution. He could not sleep twice in the same place and remain safe. One night he had to stay in a doghouse to avoid detection, with its "owner" his companion.[59]

After the War for Independence, he returned to the ruins of his home to find that his wife had died and his children were gone – nowhere to be found.

John Hart was the man who built the Baptist church of Hopewell.[60] He was a faithful member of this body of believers, and it was in this church that he and his family faithfully worshipped God and studied the Bible until the day they were scattered abroad.

Brother Joab Houghton was known as a man who had a strong mind, an inflexible will, a courageous heart, and no fear of danger. He was one of the first men[61] to advocate the calling of the Provincial Congress of New Jersey (which overthrew the British Colonial government in that state) and became one of the first members of this Assembly, representing Hunterdon County. He received one of the earliest appointments as an officer in the New Jersey militia.

On a Sunday morning while in church, one of his aides quietly slipped to his side during the preaching, and informed him of the British attack at Lexington and Concord. With a burdened and broken heart, he sat quietly through the remainder of the service.

When it ended, he quickly slipped out, mounted the great stone block in front of the church and beckoned the people to stop and hear what he had to say. He passionately retold the congregation of the *"cowardly murder at Lexington by royal troops"* and the bravery of the minutemen attempting to hold their ground. He paused, then spoke with gravity: *"Men of New Jersey, the red coats are murdering our brethren of New England! Who follows me to Boston?"*

At once, every man present shouted *"I!"* and stepped forward. Houghton became a colonel in the Continental Army once Washington took command of the Armed Forces, and he valiantly fought with his men until the end of the War.[62]

One time, during a short period of leave at home, Houghton noticed a band of Hessians plundering the houses of the Colonial men who were out fighting in the war. Knowing that the women and children were no match against these brutish mercenaries, he (along with a few old neighboring farmers) bravely yet quietly advanced on the position of these thirteen barbaric men and took them prisoner after a brief struggle.

Brother John Brown, a wealthy businessman with a fleet of over twenty vessels, was a faithful member of the First Baptist Church in Providence, Rhode Island. Though becoming a "Revolutionist" would jeopardize his trading routes and his potential business opportunities in Canada and the Caribbean, he unwaveringly joined the cause of the War in both conviction and monetary aid.

In all reality, John Brown might be said to have begun the Revolution himself. He was responsible for something called *"the Gaspée Affair,"* one of the most significant events leading up to America's War for Independence.

In 1772, the *HMS Gaspée*, along with other similar vessels, was commissioned by the British government to enforce the trade regulations that had been levied upon the American Colonies. Without any warning or warrant, her crew had full authority from the English government to inspect any vessel for contraband and stop Colonial vessels that were supposedly subverting the taxation of the British. The *Gaspée* was prepared to carry out its mission from the Crown with deadly force.

She was a constant annoyance to the mariners and ship-owners around the Narragansett Bay of Rhode Island. Her obnoxious captain William Dudingston and her crew continually imposed themselves upon the colonists, interfered with their business for no purpose, and unlawfully confiscated whatever goods they wanted to take. This infuriated John Brown and others like him, so they began to secretly discuss what could be done to stop this unnecessary and uncalled-for bullying by the British.

On June 9, 1772, late that night, the *Gaspée* ran aground in shallow water while chasing the packet boat *Hannah* that was scooting close to the Rhode Island shore. The crew was unable to free her immediately, but the quickly rising tide would soon allow the ship to free herself. However, John Brown and his fellow "Sons of Liberty" decided that they were not going to allow this to happen. They had had enough.

Around 2 A.M. the next morning, he and one of his best shipmasters Captain Abraham Whipple (who later became a leading commodore in the United States Navy during the fight for Independence), along with another 64 armed men, boarded eight of Brown's ships and sailed to the stuck *Gaspée*. As they drew close to the British vessel, shots were exchanged, and Lieutenant Dudingston was wounded. The colonists swarmed over the side of the ship and met little resistance by the British, who quickly turned and fled in dinghies or jumped overboard.

After they looted the ship and took back what had been wrongfully taken from them and their fellow colonists, Whipple and Brown were the last men on board. Without hesitation, they placed explosives throughout the ship and blew her up.[63]

This early act of defiance greatly ruffled the pompous feathers of the British government, which in turn called for the arrest of all the men involved – on the charges of treason. They demanded for these rebels to be tried in England and, if found guilty, to be given the death penalty. Though the men were never caught and British investigators were unable to obtain sufficient evidence to incriminate Brown and his men, the prospect of this happening greatly alarmed the Americans. This was one of the supreme warning signs early on that opened their eyes to how serious and vicious of a tyranny the British Empire wanted to impose upon the Colonies in order to bring them into subjection.

As a result, Samuel Adams and twenty other influential patriots formed the first *"Committee of Correspondence"* in Boston. The purpose of the Boston Committee of Correspondence was to: *"Prepare a statement of the rights of the colonists, and of this province in particular, as men, as Christians, and as subjects; prepare a declaration of the infringement of those rights; and prepare a letter to be sent to all the towns of this province and to the world."*[64]

They listed twelve specific grievances detailing the British government's superseding of the established law. In this powerful forerunner to the Declaration of Independence, they also boldly stated, *"The right to freedom being the gift of God Almighty...the rights of the Colonists as Christians...may best be understood by reading and carefully studying the institutions of The Great Law Giver and the Head of the Christian Church, which are to be found clearly written and promulgated in the New Testament."*[65]

In Boston, Pastor John Allen preached a sermon at the Second Baptist Church that utilized the *Gaspée* affair to warn listeners about greedy monarchs, corrupt judges, and conspiracies at the highest levels in the London government to bring America to its knees. *"I reverence and love my king,"* he thundered, *"but I revere the rights of an Englishman before the authority of any king upon the earth. I distinguish greatly between a king and a tyrant, a king is the guardian and trustee of the rights and laws of the people, but a tyrant destroys them."*[66]

This sermon was so powerful that it was printed seven different times in four cities and became one of the most popular pamphlets of Colonial America. It was one of the literary pieces that awoke the colonialists from a lull of inactivity in 1772.

By late 1773, each colony had followed suit and begun its own central Committee of Correspondence. These committees were designed to coordinate political strategies between the thirteen colonies and served as provisional state governments. These Committees of Correspondence were the predecessors to the First and Second Continental Congresses.

The Gaspée Affair with Brother John Brown was the catalyst that brought our Founding Fathers to action.

Conclusion

Thousands of Bible believers from all thirteen colonies swelled the ranks of the Continental Army and diligently labored for the triumph of the Revolution with all their might. They earned for themselves in that generation a reputation for love of country and valor.

The Baptists were thoroughly involved in the fight for freedom; those who could not serve in the Army did their part at home to provide supplies and to continually plant the seeds of patriotism in the hearts of those who questioned the cause when times were bleak and hard.

Where could we begin with all the stories of sacrifice and how could we tell of the numerous heroic acts that our dear brethren accomplished on the fields of battle? So many men gave up the comforts of home so that their families and future descendants could see a better tomorrow.

Thousands of names should be listed here and thousands of stories should be described; but, because of the lack of human records, they cannot be mentioned. However, one day in Heaven, we will finally be privileged to meet this countless host of Independent Baptist men and women who gave their last full measure of devotion for the cause of freedom.

The Highest of Commendations

Our Baptist forefathers did not engage themselves in the struggle of freedom for public acclamation or commendation. Rather, they put their all on the line because they simply believed what they had been called upon to do was the will of God in Heaven. Though many of them were not advocates for bloodshed, they still unashamedly and wholeheartedly pursued this higher calling, understanding that liberty and the lives of their families were worth fighting for.

Nevertheless, their public character, their ardent patriotism for America, and their courage in the field of battle caught the eye of many Founding Fathers.

Robert Howison, a notable secular historian of Virginia from the 1800s, relates, *"No class of the people of America were more devoted advocates of the principles of the Revolution, none were more willing to give their money and goods to their country, none more prompt to march to the field of battle, and none more heroic in actual conflict than the Baptist."*[67]

Thomas Jefferson had a special regard for the Baptists. Occasionally in his letters, he would sometimes scorn and criticize other denominations, but in all the documents of his that we can find, there is not one unfriendly word to or about the Baptists.

Furthermore, writing about the Baptist denomination, he said, *"We have acted together from the origin to the end of a memorable Revolution, and we have contributed, each in a line allotted us, our endeavors to render its issue a permanent blessing to our country. That our social intercourse may, to the evening of our days, be cheered and cemented by witnessing the freedom and happiness for which we have labored, will be my constant prayer. Accept the offering of my affectionate esteem and respect."*[68]

In 1856, historian Thomas Curtis accounts with the recollection of Mrs. James Madison that *"there was a small Baptist church which held its monthly meetings for business at a short distance from Mr. Jefferson's house. Mr. Jefferson attended these meetings for several months in succession. The pastor on one occasion asked him how he was pleased with their church government. Mr. Jefferson replied that it struck him with great force and had interested him much, that he considered it the only form of true democracy then existing in the world, and had concluded that it would be the best plan of government for the American colonies."*[69] This was about eight to ten years before he penned the Declaration of Independence. Jefferson greatly admired the zeal and courage of Bible-believing Baptists and envisioned a republic styled after the order of their church.

John Adams, though at odds with them at times, exclusively and without bias gave the Baptists considerable credit for being the ones instrumental in swinging Delaware from stringent British loyalty to a position of passionate patriotism in favor of the War for Independence.[70]

Patrick Henry, though he was born and raised a Presbyterian, was honored to stand with the Baptist brethren on multiple occasions. He considered them his friends and the unwavering friend to the truest definition of liberty.[71]

George Washington proudly wrote that independent Baptist chaplains in the Continental Army were *"the most prominent and useful in the Army."*[72] Furthermore, after the Constitution was penned, he wrote, *"I recollect, with satisfaction, that the* [Baptist] *has been, throughout America, uniformly and almost unanimously the firm friends of civil liberty, and the persevering promoters of our glorious Revolution. I cannot hesitate to believe that they will be the faithful supporters of a free, yet efficient, general government.*"[3]

With the testimonies from such noble patriots, may we, as Bible-believing Baptists, never degenerate in our patriotism and fervor for the United States of America. In our generation, may we uncompromisingly stand up for what is right and be stellar examples of Christ. Let us be men and women of righteous character, who present to this world what it means to be a true Bible-believing Christian. Let us live up to the legacy that our brethren before us maintained!

The Formulation of National Documents

The United States of America has been greatly blessed with three matchless founding documents – the Declaration of Independence, the Constitution, and the Bill of Rights. They were unprecedented in their time; and since then, they have effectively and accurately guided us over the past two centuries. They have also given inspiration to nations around the world for a taste of three things we hold dear and three things that have been guaranteed to us as citizens – life, liberty, and the pursuit of happiness.

God used our Baptist forefathers to both indirectly and directly be instrumental in the development, adoption and ratification of these precious documents. If it were not for faithful men of God who stood up and acted upon their Bible-based beliefs, would our beloved nation have developed into something else? Would it have fallen back into the tyranny of Great Britain? Would America even be in existence today?

THE DECLARATION OF INDEPENDENCE

When our Founding Fathers signed the Declaration of Independence on July 4, 1776, they gave America its "birth certificate" and clearly spelled out our foundational principles of liberty, justice, and dependency upon God. These things are no doubt what caused this nation to rise so quickly to global prominence in just a few short years.

Thomas Jefferson, the penman of the Declaration of Independence, was indirectly influenced by the writings of an anonymous Baptist minister in England in 1620 and by Roger Williams of Rhode Island.

Thomas Jefferson mentioned in his memoirs that when he composed the Declaration of Independence, the principles within the document were not original to him, but were instead, *"intended to be an expression of the American mind."*[4]

Many historians believe that Jefferson received these ideas and principles from the writings of John Locke. However, forty-five years *before* Locke, the widely read American Baptist preacher, Roger Williams, penned the exact concepts that we find in our Declaration of Independence. Interestingly, *both* men – John Locke and Roger Williams – were heavily influenced by the writings of an anonymous Baptist minister who had been imprisoned for his faith and convictions about religious liberty in England around 1620.

It is believed that this pastor, while incarcerated in Newgate prison, was responsible for writing a petition entitled *"A Most Humble Supplication."* He smuggled his work on parchment stuffed into milk bottles to an outside contact. The message itself was written in milk and could only be read through browning the parchment by candle flame. It was transcribed and submitted to the king of England. Both the King and Parliament ignored his pleas. But the common people heard, and God used these truths to begin the framework for religious freedom in a new nation to be called the United States of America.

Notice the similarities between the thoughts of Pastor Williams and the principles of liberty found within the Declaration of Independence signed by the forefathers!

Roger Williams wrote, *"First, whereas they say, that the Civill order may erect and establish what forme of civill Government may seem in wisedome most meet, I acknowledge the proposition to be most true, both in* itself, and also considered with the end of it, that a civill Government is an Ordinance of God, to conserve the civill peace of people, so farre as concerns their Bodies and Goods, as formerly hath beene said.

"But from the Grant I infer, that the Soveraigne, originall, and foundation of civill power lies in the people, (whom they must needs meane by the civill power distinct from the Government set up.) And if so, that a People may erect and establish what forme of Government seemes to them most meete for their civill condition: It is evident that such Governments as are by them erected and established, have no more power, nor for no longer time, then the civill power or people consenting and agreeing shall betrust them with. This is cleere not only in Reason, but in the experience of all common-weales, where the people are not deprived of their naturall freedome by the power of the Tyrants."[5]

Now carefully read what Thomas Jefferson wrote in the Declaration of Independence: *"We hold these truths to be self-evident, that all men are created equal, that they are endowed by their Creator with certain unalienable Rights, that among these are Life, Liberty and the pursuit of Happiness. That to secure these rights, Governments are instituted among Men, deriving their just powers from the consent of the governed,... That whenever any Form of Government becomes destructive of these ends, it is the Right of the People to alter or to abolish it, and to institute new*

Government, laying its foundation on such principles and organizing its powers in such form, as to them shall seem most likely to effect their Safety and Happiness."

THE CONSTITUTION

Our Constitution is America's supreme set of laws written in one document setting forth the principles on which our government is to be conducted and operated. No one is above it or equal to it. All citizens (including the President, Congress, and Supreme Court justices) are bound to follow it and uphold it – not change it or reinterpret it. It has been our political formula for national success, liberty, and abundant prosperity. It is a document that was based upon Biblical principles. Thus far in our history, it has not granted but has guaranteed us our way of life and has made us the most unique nation in the world over the past 220 years.

Our Founding Fathers developed the Constitution in the light of the Declaration of Independence. The Constitution was written in relation to our nation's birth certificate for a two-fold purpose: to ensure those principles of freedom stated in our Declaration and to fix the grievances that we made toward Great Britain and its tyranny so that they would not happen in our country with our government. The Declaration of Independence expresses *why* we are who we are as a country, and the Constitution explains *how* we can continue in liberty and prosperity.

Once the Constitution was written in 1787, thirteen copies of it were distributed to the thirteen states. Each state held a convention comprised of elected delegates who would examine and debate whether it should be ratified into law or rejected.

In Massachusetts, the Convention to ratify the Constitution assembled on January 9, 1788 and was composed of nearly four hundred members (we briefly mentioned this meeting in the previous chapter). Since the American Revolution had begun in this state, the eyes of the entire nation were upon these men. Their deliberations and ultimate decision concerning the new "plan of government" the Constitution Convention in Philadelphia had drawn up would critically sway the direction of the rest of the country.

The parties for and against the Constitution were about equal. Many had mixed feelings, and others were unsure of how solid its untried political structure would hold up over the years. For you see, the tri-fold system had never been proven. It was the first of its kind, and was considered an "experiment of liberty."

Our Founding Fathers wanted to establish a government with three branches, derived from the Divine roles of Jehovah God Himself, as found in Isaiah 33:22: *"For the LORD is our judge* (the judicial branch), *the LORD is our lawgiver* (the legislative branch), *the LORD is our king* (the executive branch); *he will save us."* Among these three branches, they realized they needed to have "separation of powers" (all three branches of government are separate from each other; however, none are independent, but all are accountable to the people) because of what the Bible says in Jeremiah 17:9 – *"The heart is deceitful above all things, and desperately wicked: who can know it?"* Our forefathers knew the wickedness of their own hearts and therefore decided to implement a system of checks and balances into our Constitution to secure liberty and republicanism in the generations to follow.

The debates lasted for a month, and they were carried on with great earnestness. Things did not look favorable to Massachusetts's endorsement of the Constitution. It was during these pivotal days that three influential Baptist pastors in the state teamed up together to individually meet with the Convention's delegates and convince them that nothing but our new Constitution could politically save our country.

You see, once our founding fathers declared their independence in 1776, they set up our government with an initial "constitution" called the Articles of Confederation. The thirteen colonies ratified it by 1777.

Over ten years under its government, things were not working out as expected. The Articles of Confederation was weak in its power. It allowed the states to carry on more individually rather than united as one nation with one central government.

Some of its strong points were that it allowed Congress to raise armies, to declare war, and to sign treaties; but it did not allow Congress to raise revenue through taxes or regulate trade and collect tariffs. This resulted in much division and individualism in the colonies. The thirteen different colonies acted more as if they were thirteen different "countries" – with thirteen different currencies, thirteen different foreign policies, thirteen different tariffs, etc.

With our government spinning its wheels, financially broke and with its hands tied, our Founding Fathers had joined together once again in the same place, Independence Hall in Philadelphia where they had collaborated on the Declaration of Independence. They gathered at this Constitutional Convention to see if they could form a more perfect union. The time had come. The need was very great.

James Manning, Samuel Stillman, and Isaac Backus tirelessly spent two weeks attending the Massachusetts convention, and exerted themselves to the utmost in persuading their brethren to support the Constitution.

When the final meeting came to order, Massachusetts adopted the Constitution by a majority of nineteen votes. Though it was not a landslide victory, this pivotal decision carried considerable weight in the debates of the others.

Governor John Hancock, the president of the convention, was so overjoyed with this that he invited James Manning to close the meeting in prayer and thanksgiving to Almighty God.[76]

THE BILL OF RIGHTS

The *"Bill of Rights"* is the first Ten Amendments to the Constitution, which contains some of the most precious liberties we enjoy as Americans.

As we studied in a previous chapter, God's men intensely fought for freedom and debated the points of liberty in Independence Hall and Continental Congress. Their preaching was responsible for setting aflame the hearts of the American people for independence and freedom. One such preacher that made an incredible difference for all Americans was a pastor by the name of John Leland. Leland was a champion of religious liberty and one of the most influential Baptist preachers in Virginia. As our new nation was formed, he was highly concerned with the preservation of our freedoms. He (along with a majority of other Baptists) was concerned that the freedoms so many had sacrificed their lives for were successfully promised, protected, and preserved.[77]

As James Madison began his campaign to become a Virginia delegate for the convention ratifying our Constitution, he received a letter from Captain Joseph Spencer (a Baptist and Revolutionary War veteran who had been imprisoned during the Virginia persecutions that Madison had witnessed as a young college graduate in Orange County). He encouraged Madison to speak with Pastor John Leland and gain the support of this significant Baptist leader of the state.[78]

The two men were able to meet and discussed Madison's candidacy. During their conversation, Leland expressed the importance of the freedom of religion, the freedom of the press, the freedom of speech and other individual rights that were based upon the Bible.

Madison promised Leland that if he were elected, he would do everything in his power to see these freedoms and more incorporated into the Constitution by amendment.[79] True to his word, after his election, Madison drafted and introduced the first ten amendments to our Constitution, which have become known as the Bill of Rights.

THE DANBURY BAPTISTS

Speaking from the steps of the United States Capitol in 1920 to 15,000 people in the open air, Texas Baptist pastor George W. Truett declared: *"'Render unto Caesar the things that are Caesar's, and unto God the things that are God's,'* is one of the most revolutionary and history-making utterances that ever fell from those lips Divine. That utterance, once and for all, marked the divorcement of church and state... It was the sunrise of a new day, the echoes of which are to go on and on until in every land, whether great or small, the doctrine shall have absolute supremacy everywhere of a free church in a free state."

Since the 1960s, the liberties and freedoms of Americans have been under strong attack.

Unfortunately, modern day liberals and atheists have distorted everything our Founding Fathers believed and are now clamoring for the removal of any emphasis of Christianity and God, saying that it is unconstitutional – when in all reality, as we have clearly seen, it is not. A majority of our Founding Fathers – George Washington, John Hancock, Benjamin Rush, Thomas Jefferson, Charles Carroll, John Witherspoon, Benjamin Franklin, James McHenry, Gouverneur Morris, Patrick Henry, and many others – believed that Christianity and religion were the most important sources of liberty and were key for our government to continue.

John Jay, our first Supreme Court Justice, clearly instructed and warned, *"No human society has ever been able to maintain both order and freedom, both cohesiveness and liberty **apart from** the moral precepts of the Christian Religion applied and accepted by all the classes. Should our Republic ever forget this fundamental precept of governance, men are certain to shed their responsibilities for licentiousness and this great experiment will then surely be doomed."*[80] Our Founding Fathers clearly understood that if government was SEPARATED from Christianity – it would *"surely be doomed."*

In our current generation, the phrase "separation of church and state" has become the rallying cry for liberal groups and godless Americans to keep the church out of government and sterilize the public of any emphasis from Christianity. If this course is continued, America is surely setting itself up for disaster.

Over 65% of Americans assume that the wording "separation of church and state" is in the Constitution, but they are misinformed. Those words are not there at all. Actually, our First Amendment only says: *"Congress shall make no law respecting an establishment of religion, or prohibiting the free exercise thereof."*

The idea of separation of church and state came from correspondence between Thomas Jefferson and a group of Baptists. On October 7, 1801, the Danbury Baptist Association of Connecticut sent a letter to President Jefferson expressing their concern about religious liberty under the First Amendment. In their letter they emphasized that the freedom of religion was a right given to a human being by God and not by a government. Concerned that the government might someday wrongly believe that it *did* have the power to tell religions and churches what to do, the Danbury Baptists wanted assurance and clarification from the President that this would never happen.

On January 1, 1802, Jefferson wrote back to the Danbury Baptists. He expressed that he understood their concerns and agreed with them that a man's religion was between him and God – not government. Then, he assured them that the United States government would not infringe on those rights. Jefferson stated, *"Believing with you that religion is a matter which lies solely between man and God, I contemplate with sovereign reverence that act of the whole American people which declared that their legislature should 'make no law respecting an establishment of religion or prohibiting the free exercise thereof,' thus building a wall of separation between Church and State."*

The Danbury Baptists did not write to Jefferson because they believed him to be the only expert of the Constitution or of the First Amendment – but rather because he was the President of the United States at the time! Today, unfortunately, Thomas Jefferson is viewed as the sole spokesman and authority of the First Amendment because he wrote the words "Separation between Church and State." But Jefferson actually did not play a role in the formulation of the Constitution nor was he a "moving force" behind the creation of the Bill of Rights, as many claim him to be! As we saw earlier, the First Amendment was primarily the doing of John Leland and James Madison.

Jefferson was an ambassador in France at the time when the Constitution was written. He was not part of the Constitutional Convention, and due to such slow communication by way of letter, even if he had tried to send any suggestions to the delegation, it would have taken weeks for his notes to arrive.

His only true involvement was a private letter from overseas to one personal friend – not an open letter to the assembly. *"On receiving it* [the Constitution while in France] *I wrote strongly to Mr. Madison, urging the want of provision for the freedom of religion* [notice that it was not freedom FROM religion], *freedom of the press, trial by jury, habeas corpus, the substitution of militia for a standing army, and an express reservation to the States of all rights not specifically granted to the Union. This is all the hand I had in what related to the Constitution."*[81]

Jefferson's letter to the Danbury Baptists was not a public policy paper – it was personal and private. It was not intended to be used as law or as a standard in our court system. Furthermore, if it should be utilized in any situation, it should be used in its entirety – not taken out of context or warped to present something contrary to what was originally intended.

Thomas Jefferson also said, *"I am for freedom of religion, and against all maneuvers to bring about a legal ascendancy of one sect over another."*[82] Our Founding Fathers did not want the government to interfere with religions and churches; rather, they wanted Christianity to have freedom to flourish in America!

They believed that the United States government would only continue in prosperity and success if it followed the guide and principles of Christianity, the

Bible, and the Ten Commandments. James Madison declared, *"We have staked the whole future of American civilization, not upon the power of government, far from it. We have staked the future... upon the capacity of each and all of us to govern ourselves, to sustain ourselves, according to the Ten Commandments of God."*[83] They *wanted* Christianity to influence the government!

Benjamin Rush also understood this and was very clear in all his writings that Christianity, with *"all its doctrines and precepts are calculated to promote the happiness of society, and the safety and well being of civil government."*[84] Furthermore, he stated, *"I have always considered Christianity as the strong ground of republicanism. The spirit is opposed, not only to the splendor, but even to the very forms of monarchy, and many of its precepts have for their objects republican liberty and equality as well as simplicity, integrity, and economy in government. It is only necessary for republicanism to ally itself to the Christian religion to overturn all the corrupted political institutions..."*[85]

John Marshall, an influential statesman, Supreme Court Judge, and United States representative during the early days of America, wrote, *"The American population is entirely Christian, and with us Christianity and Religion are identified. It would be strange indeed, if with such a people, our institutions did not presuppose Christianity, and did not often refer to it, and exhibit relations with it."*[86]

However, they did not want any one specific denomination or religion (i.e. Catholic, Anglican, etc.) gaining control of the government and forcing its specific views upon society. Nevertheless, *they intended and wanted Bible-believing Christians to be involved with government as a whole and wanted BIBLE-BELIEVING CHRISTIANITY to influence its dealings.*

The founding fathers did not want a single federal denomination to rule America (*'Congress shall make no law respecting the establishment of religion...'*), but they did expect Biblical principles and values to be present throughout public life and society to ultimately influence government (*'...nor prohibiting the free exercise thereof'*).[87]

On January 19, 1853, the United States Supreme Court released the following statement: *"They intended, by this amendment, to prohibit 'an establishment of religion' such as the English Church presented, or any thing like it. But they had no fear of religion itself, nor did they wish to see us an irreligious people. They did not intend to spread over all the public authorities and the whole public action of the nation the dead and revolting spectacle of atheistic apathy. Not so had the battles of the Revolution been fought and the deliberations of the Revolutionary Congress been conducted."*

The Supreme Court in Massachusetts wrote firmly in 1838: *"The First Amendment embraces all who believe in the existence of God, as well as Christians of every denomination. This provision does not extend to atheists, because they do not believe in God or religion; and therefore their sentiments and professions, whatever they may be, cannot be called religious sentiments and professions."*[88] Therefore, we clearly see that according to what the Supreme Court believed, the First Amendment does not and cannot apply to atheists or non-religious individuals, since they do not believe in God or "religion" at all! They understood that atheism was infidelity – NOT a religion – and ultimately had no right to barge in to and abuse the protected freedom of Christians or religious people.

The first United States Supreme Court cases ever to consider the usage of the phrase "separation of church and state" from Jefferson's letter did not take those words out of context. Rather, they used the phrase in conjunction with the entirety of the letter and its intent.

Of course, all men are under the law and should obey the law; and obviously, religious institutions and denominations were not exempt from that! The Supreme Court declared in 1859 and 1878, *"Congress was deprived of all legislative power over mere religious opinion, but was left free to reach only those religious actions which were in violation of social duties or subversive of good order. The rightful purposes of civil government are for its officers to interfere ONLY when religious principles break out into overt acts against peace and good order. In this is found the true distinction between what properly belongs to the church and what to the State."*[89]

The Supreme Court believed that the government had no right to interfere with the Church whatsoever unless crimes were committed in the name of religion or something morally unlawful was done (such as human sacrifice, polygamy, bigamy, having concubines, incest, injury to children, promotion of immorality, etc.). Common sense makes it clear that in such cases, the governmental authorities should intervene.

However, in all other areas – even in the areas of public prayers, public preaching, public singing, and the distribution of Gospel literature – the Supreme Court declared that the government had no right to interfere.

Unfortunately, the First Amendment is now being used to PROHIBIT the very religious activities that the Founding Fathers once ENCOURAGED under the same amendment. Modern-day liberals and atheists have distorted everything our Founding Fathers believed and are now trying to clamor for the removal of any emphasis of Christianity and God, saying that it is unconstitutional – when in all reality, it is not.

Separation of church and state? YES. The government should stay out of the specific dealings of the church as long as the church does not promote actions that are "subversive of good order"; however, Christianity is encouraged to take part in the government as long as a specific denomination does not take control and force its specific "religion" on everyone else.

In Thomas Jefferson's letter, he explained that the First Amendment of the Constitution put a WALL up to block the government from infringing upon the rights of religion and Christianity, but put no such hindrance on the church – the opposite of how it is viewed and interpreted today!

Conclusion

At the conclusion of the War for Independence, Isaac Backus summarized the excitement of what all Baptists believed about their newly birthed country: *"America is reserved in the mind of Jehovah to be the grand theater on which the divine Redeemer will accomplish glorious things."*[90] God did have great things in store for what He wanted our unique nation to accomplish.

America became the hope of countless people across the world seeking religious freedom and political asylum. She became the example to other nations of what true liberty meant. Many followed in her footsteps and were able to shake off the bonds of tyranny.

What other nation in the history of the world has done more for the kingdom of God? By the 1850s, America had already sent out thousands of missionaries evangelizing all regions of the globe. When our country was formed, the United States became the lighthouse to the lost, the bulwark of Bible-believing Christianity, and the heart of revival fires that spread into Europe, Asia, and Africa.

Indeed, our country is a miracle of progress unmatched in the annals of history. And as Baptists, we have an incredible heritage in how our ancestors helped make our country a reality. So many of our brothers made a profound influence upon America and played an instrumental role in the formulation of our great nation!

I am proud to be an American. I am proud to be a Bible-believing Christian. But, I am proud to be a Baptist!

ENDNOTES

[1] *The Trail of Blood* by J. M. Carroll, Lecture V., Point VI.
[2] Hildreth's *History of the United States*, N.Y., I., 497-499.
[3] Cramp's *History of the Baptists*, page 532.
[4] Howison's *History of Virginia*, II., pages 167-168.
[5] *History of the Rise and Progress of the Baptists in Virginia* by Robert Semple, 1810, page 19.
[6] Howison's *History of Viriginia*, II., page 169.
[7] Ibid.
[8] *History of the Rise and Progress of the Baptists in Virginia* by Robert Semple, 1810, page 19.
[9] Leland's *Works*, page 107.
[10] Howe's *Virginia Historical Collections*, page 239, Charleston, 1846.
[11] Howison's *History of Virginia*, II., page 169, Richmond, 1848.
[12] Leland's *Works*, page 107.
[13] Semple's *History of Virginia Baptists*, page 21.
[14] *History of the Ketocton Baptist Association* by William Fristoe, 1808, page 69.
[15] *History of the Protestant Episcopal Church of Virginia* by Francis Hawks, 1836, page 121.

[16] Backus' *Church History*, Newton, II., page 97.
[17] Ibid., pages 94-95, note.
[18] *Collections of the Rhode Island Historical Society*, VI., by Morgan Edwards, page 304.
[19] Arnold's *History of Rhode Island*, II., page 563.
[20] *Collections of the Rhode Island Historical Society*, VI., by Morgan Edwards, page 304.
[21] Walter B. Shurden, *How We Got that Way*, pamphlet published by the Baptist Joint Committee on Public Affairs, page 8.
[22] Bancroft's *History of the United States*, V., page 218.
[23] *Biography of the Signers of the Declaration of Independence*, Philadelphia, 1831, I., page 341.
[24] Sabine's *American Loyalists*, Boston, 1847, page 15.
[25] *History of the United States*, IX., page 261.
[26] *Biography of the Signers of the Declaration of Independence*, Philadelphia, 1831, I., page 374; Arnold's *History of Rhode Island*, N.Y., 1860, II., page 374.
[27] Howison's *History of Virginia*, II., page 133.
[28] Bancroft's *History of the United States*, IX., page 36.
[29] *History of England* by Hume, Smollett, and Farr, III., page 99.
[30] *Collections of the Rhode Island Historical Society*, VI., page 290.
[31] *Biography of the Signers of the Declaration of Independence*, I., page 373.
[32] Backus' *History of the Baptists*, Newton, II., page 200, note.
[33] *Minutes of Philadelphia Baptist Association*, page 460.
[34] Headley's *Chaplains and Clergy of the Revolution*, page 250, N.Y., 1864.
[35] Semple's *History of the Virginia Baptists*, page 62.
[36] Ibid.
[37] Howe's *Virginia Historical Collections*, page 238.
[38] Sprague's *Annals of the American Baptist Pulpit*, page 134.
[39] *Manning and Brown University*, pages 137-138, Boston.
[40] http://en.wikipedia.org/wiki/Isles_of_Shoals

[41] *Manning and Brown University,* page 94.
[42] Headley's *Chaplains and Clergy of the Revolution,* page 255.
[43] Ibid, page 257.
[44] Ibid.
[45] Ibid, page 18.
[46] *Manning and Brown University,* page 136, Boston, 1864.
[47] *Virginia Historical Collections,* page 238.
[48] Sprague's *Annals of the American Baptist Pulpit,* page 92.
[49] *Manning and Brown University,* pages 259-260.
[50] *The Chaplains and Clergy of the Revolution* by J.T. Headley, page 4.
[51] Inscribed on Panel Three within the Jefferson Memorial in Washington D.C.
[52] Semple's *History of the Virginia Baptists,* page 359.
[53] Ibid., 372.
[54] Sprague's *Annals of the American Baptist Pulpit,* pages 48-49.
[55] Ibid., 162.
[56] Ibid., 78.
[57] Frank Moore, editor, *The Patriot Preachers of the American Revolution, with Biographical Sketches,* 1860, pages 258-288.
[58] *Biography of the Signers of the Declaration of Independence,* Philadelphia, 1831, III., page 256.
[59] *Historical Collections of New Jersey,* page 262, New York, 1847.
[60] *The Book of the Signers of the Declaration of Independence,* Philadelphia, 1861, pages 35-36.
[61] *Life of Dr. Cone,* New York, 1856, page 11.
[62] Ibid.
[63] Manning and Brown University, pages 170-171.
[64] *The Rights of the Colonists* by Samuel Adams. The Report of the Committee of Correspondence to the Boston Town Meeting, November 20, 1772.
[65] Ibid.
[66] *An Oration Upon the Beauties of Liberty* by John Allen. New

London, 1773. In Ellis Sandoz, ed., *Political Sermons of the American Founding Era*, 1730-1805 2nd edition. (Indianapolis, 1998), 1: page 307.

[67] *The History of Virginia* by Robert Howison, Volume II, page 170.

[68] *Jefferson's Complete Works*, by Washington, N. Y., Volume VIII, page 168.

[69] *The Process of Baptist Principles in the Last Hundred Years* by Thomas Fenner Curtis, 1856, page 356-357.

[70] *Life and Works of John Adams* by Charles Francis, (Boston: Little, Brown, and Co.,) Volume X, page 812.

[71] *The History of Virginia* by Robert Howison, page 168.

[72] *Manning and Brown University*, page 136, Boston, 1864.

[73] *Writings of George Washington*, compiled by Jared Sparks, Volume XII, printed in Boston, pages 154-155.

[74] Letter from Thomas Jefferson to Richard Henry Lee in 1825.

[75] Roger Williams, *The Complete Writings of Roger Williams, Vol. 3, The Bloudy Tenet of Persecution*, p. 249-250.

[76] The American Quarterly Register, Volume 11, printed 1839, page 350.

[77] Letter from Captain Joseph Spencer to James Madison on February 28, 1788.

[78] *Elder John Leland, Jeffersonian Itinerant*, by L.H. Butterfield, (printed 1952), pages 155 and 185.

[79] *The Fourth President: A Life of James Madison* by Irving Brant, (printed 1970), pages 222-224.

[80] From Address to the American Bible Society on May 9, 1822, by John Jay. Also recorded in *The Correspondence and Public Papers of John Jay, Vol. IV*, page 484.

[81] Letter from Thomas Jefferson to Dr. Joseph Priestley on June 19, 1802.

[82] Letter from Thomas Jefferson to Elbridge Gerry on January 26, 1799.

[83] *America's God and Country: Encyclopedia of Quotations* by

William Federer, 1994, page 411.
[84] *"Essays, Literary, Moral and Philosophical* by Dr. Benjamin Rush, 1798, page 8, "Of the Mode of Education Proper in a Republic," Calling for free public schools in 1790.
[85] Letter from Dr. Benjamin Rush to Thomas Jefferson on August 22, 1800.
[86] Letter from Chief Justice Marshall to Jasper Adams on May 9, 1833.
[87] http://www.davidbarton.net/2010/02/12/separation-of-church-state-part-two-by-david-barton/; See also *Separation of Church and State: What the Founders Meant,* by David Barton, Aledo, Tex.: WallBuilder Press., 2007.
[88] *America's God and Country: Encyclopedia of Quotations* by William Federer, 1994, page 432.
[89] United States Supreme Court Case, *Reynolds v. United States,* 98 U.S. 145, 1878. See also *Separation of Church and State: What the Founders Meant,* by David Barton, Aledo, Tex.: WallBuilder Press., 2007.
[90] Warren Association, *Minutes of the Warren Association,* Boston, 1784, pages 6-7.
[91] Adapted from *The Baptist Encyclopedia,* 1881.

John Gano preaching and praying after the final victory at the Battle of Yorktown.

WHAT WE BELIEVE

George W. Truett, famed pastor of the First Baptist Church of Dallas, declared a century ago: *"Every Baptist ought to know why he is a Baptist, and to know it from the specific commands of God's Word. Not to have such knowledge is for our churches to be harmed in every way."*

Throughout the Word of God, our Lord places a great emphasis upon knowing what we believe and why we believe it and understanding Bible doctrine. II Timothy 2:15 admonishes us, *"Study to shew thyself approved unto God, a workman that needeth not to be ashamed, rightly dividing the word of truth."* II Peter 3:18 encourages us to *"grow in grace, and in the knowledge of our Lord and Saviour Jesus Christ."* I Timothy 4:13-16 instructs us, *"...give attendance to reading, to exhortation, to doctrine. Meditate upon these things; give thyself wholly to them; that thy profiting may appear to all... Take heed to thyself, and unto the doctrine."* Did you notice the imperative verbs in the verses you just read? God clearly commanded us to study His Word *"that the man of God may be perfect* [mature], *thoroughly furnished unto all good works"* (II Timothy 3:17). Plainly put, the study of God's Word is not optional for the Christian.

Nevertheless, God eagerly wants His people to have the desire to diligently ever increase in their familiarity with the Scriptures – because it is through the Word of God that we can become more familiar with Him, His Will for our lives, His work through our lives, and the way He operates in our lives. Truly, what *"joy unspeakable and full of glory"* (I Peter 1:8) any Christian should be overwhelmed with as each of us realizes that we GET to know more about God – His principles and precepts to guide us into all truth, His purpose for our existence, His plan for our lives, His provision of salvation, His pardon of our sins, and His preparation of our Home in Glory. This is not just a god – a false god made by man's hands or created by man's imagination – this is the God of Heaven!

The doctrines of the Bible can be divided into 9 basic categories:

1. BIBLIOLOGY – the doctrine of the Bible
2. THEOLOGY – the doctrine of God
3. CHRISTOLOGY – the doctrine of Christ
4. PNEUMATOLOGY – the doctrine of the Holy Spirit

5. ANTHROPOLOGY – the doctrine of man
6. SOTERIOLOGY – the doctrine of salvation
7. ECCLESIOLOGY – the doctrine of the church
8. ANGELOLOGY – the doctrine of angels
9. ESCHATOLOGY – the doctrine of last things

Volumes have been written about what the Bible teaches. I highly encourage you to ask your pastor for his recommendation of a good book that could give you an in-depth study of Bible doctrines. Learn for yourself what we believe, based on Scripture, so that you might *"be ready always to give an answer to every man that asketh you a reason for the hope that is in you"* (I Peter 3:15).

Here is a list of the Fundamentals of the faith and the Baptist distinctives – the Bible principles that have set the Baptists apart from other religions and denominations. I encourage you to take your Bible and study each of these truths for yourself. Understand what we believe and why we believe it.

There are many verses throughout the Bible that prove each doctrinal statement given, but here are just a few to initially help you on your study of why we are Baptists.

The Fundamentals of the Faith

I. We believe in the **verbal plenary inspiration of Scripture,** that every word and every part of the Bible is God-breathed and written by the Holy Ghost through His men.

> II Timothy 3:16-17, *"All Scripture is given by inspiration of God, and is profitable for doctrine, for reproof, for correction, for instruction in righteousness: That the man of God may be perfect, thoroughly furnished unto all good works."*
>
> II Peter 1:21, *"For the prophecy came not in old time by the will of man: but holy men of God spake as they were moved by the Holy Ghost."*
>
> John 17:17, *"Sanctify them through thy truth: thy word is truth."*

II. We believe in the **deity of Christ.**

> John 1:1-3 & 14, *"In the beginning was the Word, and the Word was with God, and the Word was God. The same was in the beginning with God. All things were made by him; and without him was not any thing made that was made. And the Word was made flesh, and dwelt among us, (and we beheld his glory, the glory as of the only begotten of the Father,) full of grace and truth."*

III. We believe in the **virgin birth of Christ.**

> Matthew 1:18-25, *"Now the birth of Jesus Christ was on this wise: When as his mother Mary was espoused to Joseph, before they came together, she was found with child of the Holy Ghost. Then Joseph*

her husband, being a just man, and not willing to make her a public example, was minded to put her away privily. But while he thought on these things, behold, the angel of the Lord appeared unto him in a dream, saying, Joseph, thou son of David, fear not to take unto thee Mary thy wife; for that which is conceived in her is of the Holy Ghost. And she shall bring forth a son, and thou shalt call his name JESUS: for he shall save his people from their sins. Now all this was done, that it might be fulfilled which was spoken of the Lord by the prophet, saying, Behold, a virgin shall be with child, and shall bring forth a son, and they shall call his name Emmanuel, which being interpreted is, God with us. Then Joseph being raised from sleep did as the angel of the Lord had bidden him, and took unto him his wife: And knew her not till she had brought forth her firstborn son: and he called his name JESUS."

Isaiah 7:14, *"Therefore the Lord himself shall give you a sign; Behold, a virgin shall conceive, and bear a son, and shall call his name Immanuel."*

IV. We believe in the **vicarious substitutionary death of Christ.**

Romans 5:8, *"But God commendeth his love toward us, in that, while we were yet sinners, Christ died for us."*

II Corinthians 5:21, *"For he hath made him to be*

sin for us, who knew no sin; that we might be made the righteousness of God in him."

John 3:16, "For God so loved the world, that he gave his only begotten Son, that whosoever believeth in him should not perish, but have everlasting life."

II Corinthians 8:9, "For ye know the grace of our Lord Jesus Christ, that, though he was rich, yet for your sakes he became poor, that ye through his poverty might be rich."

V. We believe in the **visible, personal return** of Jesus Christ.

I Thessalonians 4:13-18, "But I would not have you to be ignorant, brethren, concerning them which are asleep, that ye sorrow not, even as others which have no hope. For if we believe that Jesus died and rose again, even so them also which sleep in Jesus will God bring with him. For this we say unto you by the word of the Lord, that we which are alive and remain unto the coming of the Lord shall not prevent them which are asleep. For the Lord himself shall descend from heaven with a shout, with the voice of the archangel, and with the trump of God: and the dead in Christ shall rise first: Then we which are alive and remain shall be caught up together with them in the clouds to meet the Lord in the air: and so shall we ever be with the Lord. Wherefore comfort one another with these words."

Acts 1:11, *"Which also said, Ye men of Galilee, why stand ye gazing up into heaven? this same Jesus, which is taken up from you into heaven, shall so come in like manner as ye have seen him go into heaven."*

I John 2:28, *"And now, little children, abide in him; that, when he shall appear, we may have confidence, and not be ashamed before him at his coming."*

John 14:1-3, *"Let not your heart be troubled: ye believe in God, believe also in me. In my Father's house are many mansions: if it were not so, I would have told you. I go to prepare a place for you. And if I go and prepare a place for you, I will come again, and receive you unto myself; that where I am, there ye may be also."*

VI. We believe in the **bodily resurrection of Christ**.

Matthew 28:1-7, *"In the end of the sabbath, as it began to dawn toward the first day of the week, came Mary Magdalene and the other Mary to see the sepulcher. And, behold, there was a great earthquake: for the angel of the Lord descended from heaven, and came and rolled back the stone from the door, and sat upon it. His countenance was like lightning, and his raiment white as snow: And for fear of him the keepers did shake, and became as dead men. And the angel answered and said unto the women, Fear not ye: for I know that ye seek Jesus, which was crucified. He is not here: for he is risen, as he said. Come, see the place where the Lord lay. And go quickly, and tell his disciples that he is risen from the dead; and, behold, he goeth before you into Galilee; there shall ye see him: lo, I have told you."*

VII. We believe in the **blood atonement of Christ.**

Ephesians 1:7, *"In whom we have redemption through his blood, the forgiveness of sins, according to the riches of his grace;"*

Colossians 1:13-14, *"Who hath delivered us from the power of darkness, and hath translated us into the kingdom of his dear Son: In whom we have redemption through his blood, even the forgiveness of sins:"*

VIII. We believe in **salvation by grace through faith.**

Ephesians 2:1-9, *"And you hath he quickened, who were dead in trespasses and sins Wherein in time past ye walked according to the course of this world, according to the prince of the power of the air, the spirit that now worketh in the children of disobedience: Among whom also we all had our conversation in times past in the lusts of our flesh, fulfilling the desires of the flesh and of the mind; and were by nature the children of wrath, even as others. But God, who is rich in mercy, for his great love wherewith he loved us, Even when we were dead in* *sins, hath quickened us together with Christ, by (grace ye are saved;) And hath raised us up together, and made us sit together in heavenly places in Christ Jesus: That in the ages to come he might show the exceeding riches of his grace in his kindness toward us through Christ Jesus. For by grace are ye saved through faith; and that not of yourselves: it is the gift of God: Not of works, lest any man should boast."*

THE BAPTIST DISTINCTIVES

*The Baptist distinctives are easier to remember by making an acrostic with the word "Baptists."

B – **Bible is our only authority for faith and practice.** God's Word is the sole authority in all matters because the Bible is inspired by God and bears the absolute authority of God Himself. Whatever the Bible affirms, Baptists accept as true. No human opinion or decree of any church group can override the Bible. Even creeds and confessions of faith, which attempt to articulate the theology of Scripture, do not carry Scripture's inherent authority.

> II Timothy 3:16, *"All Scripture is given by inspiration of God, and is profitable for doctrine, for reproof, for correction, for instruction in righteousness:"*

> I Peter 1:23-25, *"Being born again, not of corruptible seed, but of incorruptible, by the word of*

> *God, which liveth and abideth forever. For all flesh is as grass, and all the glory of man as the flower of grass. The grass withereth, and the flower thereof falleth away: But the word of the Lord endureth forever. And this is the word which by the gospel is preached unto you."*

> **I Thessalonians 2:13,** *"For this cause also thank we God without ceasing, because, when ye received the word of God which ye heard of us, ye received it not as the word of men, but as it is in truth, the word of God, which effectually worketh also in you that believe.*

A – Autonomy (independent self-rule) of the local church. The local church is an independent body accountable to the Lord Jesus Christ, the Head of the church. All human authority for governing the local church resides within the local church itself. Thus the church is autonomous, or self-governing. No religious hierarchy outside the local church may dictate a church's beliefs or practices. Autonomy does not mean isolation. A Baptist church may fellowship with other churches around mutual interests and in an associational tie, but a Baptist church is not a "member" of any other body.

> **Acts 6:1-7,** *"And in those days, when the number of the disciples were multiplied, there arose a murmuring of the Grecians against the Hebrews, because their widows were neglected in the daily ministration. Then the twelve called the multitude of the disciples unto them, and said, It is not reason that we should leave*

the word of God, and serve tables. Wherefore, brethren, look ye out among you seven men of honest report, full of the Holy Ghost and wisdom, whom we may appoint over this business. But we will give ourselves continually to prayer, and to the ministry of the word. And the saying pleased the whole multitude: and they chose Stephen, a man full of faith and of the Holy Ghost, and Philip, and Prochorus, and Nicanor, and Timon, and Parmenas, and Nicolas a proselyte of Antioch: Whom they set before the apostles: and when they had prayed, they laid their hands on them. And the word of God increased; and the number of the disciples multiplied in Jerusalem greatly; and a great company of the priests were obedient to the faith."

Colossians 1:18, *"And he is the head of the body, the church: who is the beginning, the firstborn from the dead; that in all things he might have the preeminence."*

P – **Priesthood of the believers.** Every born-again believer has direct access to the throne of God. Therefore, since every child of God shares in the priesthood of the believers, all have the same right as ordained ministers to communicate with God, interpret Scripture, and minister in Christ's name. Who needs a priest when we are already priests ourselves (1 Peter 2:5)? This was secured by Christ's redemptive work on the cross. We are to have *"boldness to enter the Holiest by the blood of Jesus* (Hebrews 10:19)." Furthermore, the Holy Spirit enables our access as we *"have access by one Spirit to the Father* (Ephesians

2:18)." We need no intervention by any other human being on our behalf.

> **Hebrews 10:19-20,** *"Having therefore, brethren, boldness to enter into the holiest by the blood of Jesus, By a new and living way, which he hath consecrated for us, through the veil, that is to say, his flesh;"*

> **I Peter 2:5 & 9,** *"Ye also,...are built up...an holy priesthood.... But ye are a chose generation, a royal priesthood,...that ye should show forth the praises of him who hath called you out of darkness into his marvelous light.*

T - **Two ordinances: Baptism and the Lord's Supper.** We practice believer's baptism by immersion, which is the only acceptable mode of baptism because it alone preserves the picture of saving truth. No other form of baptism pictures the death, burial, and resurrection of Christ (Romans 6:1-5). We believe that the Lord's Supper is a symbolic ordinance, picturing Christ's body broken for our sins and His blood shed for our redemption. It is not a saving ordinance, but helps us remember His death, and inspires us while looking forward to His coming. It is to be observed by regenerate, obedient believers.

> **Matthew 28:19-20,** *"Go ye therefore, and teach all nations, baptizing them in the name of the Father, and of the Son, and of the Holy Ghost: Teaching them to observe all things whatsoever I have commanded you: and, lo, I am with you always, even unto the end of*

the world. Amen."

I Corinthians 11:23-28, *"For I have received of the Lord that which also I delivered unto you, That the Lord Jesus the same night in which he was betrayed took bread: And when he had given thanks, he broke it, and said, Take, eat: this is my body, which is broken for you: this do in remembrance of me. After the same manner also he took the cup, when he had supped, saying, This cup is the new testament in my blood: this do ye, as oft as ye drink it, in remembrance of me. For as often as ye eat this bread, and drink this cup, ye do show the Lord's death till he come. Wherefore whosoever shall eat this bread, and drink this cup of the Lord, unworthily, shall be guilty of the body and blood of the Lord. But let a man examine himself, and so let him eat of that bread, and drink of that cup."*

I - **Individual freedom and responsibility.** Every individual Christian has the liberty to believe as his/her own conscience dictates. While we seek to persuade men to choose the right, a person must not be forced into compliance; every person has been created with a free will. The individual soul is answerable to Almighty God and to Him alone. This precludes giving up that independency to a pope, a priest, a system, an organization, a convention, a fellowship, an association, or any other human being. None of these are given the authority to interpose anything whatsoever between the individual believer and God concerning any matter of faith.

Baptists & the American Revolution

> I John 2:27, *"But the anointing which ye have received of him abideth in you, and ye need not that any man teach you: but as the same anointing teacheth you of all things, and is truth, and is no lie, and even as it hath taught you, ye shall abide in him."*

> Acts 5:29, *"Then Peter and the other apostles answered and said, We ought to obey God rather than men."*

> Romans 14:12, *"So then everyone of us shall give account of himself to God.*

S – **Separation of church and state.** God established both the church and the civil government, and gave each its own distinct sphere of operation. The government's purposes are outlined in Romans 13:1-7 and I Peter 2:13-14: to restrain evil and reward good. The church's ultimate purposes are outlined by Christ in Matthew 28:18-20. Neither should control the other, nor should there be an alliance between the two. Christians in a free society can properly influence government toward righteousness, which is not the same as a denomination or group of churches controlling the government.

> Matthew 22:17-22, *"Tell us therefore, What thinkest thou? Is it lawful to give tribute unto Caesar, or not? But Jesus perceived their wickedness, and said, Why tempt ye me, ye hypocrites? Show me the tribute money. And they brought unto him a penny. And he saith unto them, Whose is this image and*

superscription? They say unto him, Caesar's. Then saith he unto them, Render therefore unto Caesar the things which are Caesar's; and unto God the things that are God's. When they had heard these words, they marveled, and left him, and went their way."

Christians are to pray for and obey governmental authority *(I Timothy 2:1-4)*, unless it forbids what God requires or requires what God forbids, in which case Christians cannot submit and some form of civil disobedience becomes inescapable *(Acts 4:18-31, 5:17-29)*. Believers are also to influence government, because all of life is under God's authority *(Psalm 24:1; Psalm 83:18; Isaiah 42:8; Matthew 28:18-20; 2 Corinthians 10:5)*.

Our Founding Fathers designed our government in such a way that American citizens would be able to stand against the leadership of the country, if it ever went the wrong direction, began to abuse its powers, or exploited our liberties. Romans 13:1-4 is our authority on this.

Many Christians have read this passage and are afraid to let their voices be heard as a result of not thoroughly understanding it. The first two verses read: *"Let every soul be subject unto the higher powers. For there is no power but of God: the powers that be are ordained of God. Whosoever therefore resisteth the power, resisteth the ordinance of God: and they that resist shall receive to themselves damnation."* Many have read this passage and have equated "the higher power" with the government. **This is the wrong interpretation when applied to the system of the United States.**

In America, all men – from the President, Congressmen, and Supreme Court Justices down to the average citizen – are bound together UNDER the law. No one is exempt from it. No one is above it. No one is equal to it. The supreme law of the land and the "higher power" that our Founding Fathers instituted for all citizens to follow is THE CONSTITUTION OF THE UNITED STATES. This was based upon Biblical principles.

The Bible says in Leviticus 24:22, *"Ye shall have one manner of law, as well for the stranger, as for one of your own country: for I am the Lord your God."* Notice, **the government** is not above the law. There is to be one law for everyone. The government is to obey the laws that they are elected to uphold. God re-emphasized this point in Numbers 15:16, *"One law and one manner shall be for you, and for the stranger that sojourneth with you."* The stranger, the citizen, and the government are to all have one law by which they are to obey.

Romans 13:1 says, *"Let every soul be subject unto the higher powers. For there is no power but of God: the powers that be are ordained of God."* *"Every soul"* **includes elected officials.** If the elected official breaks the law, then they should have to pay the same price as the citizen would if they broke the law.

Re-read Romans 13:1-2 with the understanding that our Founding Fathers wisely established the Constitution as our country's highest authority: *"Let every soul be subject unto the higher powers* [The Constitution]. *For there is no power but of God: the powers that be are ordained of God* [Truly God did ordain the Constitution by "favoring them with understanding" in the Convention]. *Whosoever therefore resisteth the power* [The Constitution], *resisteth the ordinance of God: and they that resist* [The Constitution] *shall receive to themselves damnation."*

Christians are not the ones who have to worry about damnation and the judgment of God falling upon them. Rather, the liberals – who want to twist the Constitution out of context and bend it to meet their own devious, anti-God agendas – are the ones who need to beware!

Of course, citizens should not stand against our government in a spirit or attitude that would displease the Lord, but rather they should conduct themselves civilly with the character of Christ. Many believe they should pick up the musket and charge Capitol Hill. Is this really what Christ would do or what He taught us about how to handle ourselves?

When Peter acted in a hot-headed manner, Christ rebuked him by stating in Matthew 26:52-53: *"Put up again thy sword into his place: for all they that take the sword shall perish with the sword. Thinkest thou that I cannot now pray to my Father, and he shall presently give me more than twelve legions of angels?"* Was Christ attempting to use this moment to teach pacifism? Not at all. He was trying to show his disciples the importance of prayer.

T – **Two offices of the local church.** The Bible mandates only two offices in the church—pastor and deacon. The terms *pastor, elder, bishop* and *overseer* all refer to the same office. The two offices of pastor and deacon exist within the local church, not as a hierarchy outside or over the local church. —*I Timothy 3:1-7* (pastor); *I Timothy 3:8-16* (deacon)

I Timothy 3:1-16, *"This is a true saying, If a man desire the office of a bishop, he desireth a good work. A bishop then must be blameless, the husband of one wife, vigilant, sober, of good behavior, given to hospitality, apt to teach; Not given to wine, no striker, not greedy of filthy lucre; but patient, not a brawler, not covetous; One that ruleth well his own house, having his children in subjection with all gravity; (For if a man know not how to rule his own house, how shall he take care of the church of God?) Not a novice, lest being lifted up with pride he fall into the condemnation of the devil. Moreover he must have a good report of them which are without; lest he fall into reproach and the snare of the devil. Likewise must the deacons be grave, not doubletongued, not given to much wine, not greedy of filthy lucre; Holding the mystery of the faith in a pure conscience. And let these also first be proved; then let them use the office of a deacon, being found blameless. Even so must their wives be grave, not slanderers, sober, faithful in all things. Let the deacons be the husbands of one wife, ruling their children and their own houses well. For they that have used the office of a deacon well purchase to themselves a good degree, and great boldness in the faith which is in Christ Jesus. These things write I unto thee, hoping to come unto thee shortly: But if I tarry long, that thou mayest know how thou oughtest to behave thyself in the house of God, which is the church of the living God, the pillar and ground of the truth. And without controversy great is the mystery of godliness: God was manifest in the flesh, justified in the Spirit, seen of angels, preached unto the Gentiles, believed on in the world, received up into glory."*

S – **Saved and baptized church membership.** Local church membership is restricted to individuals who give a believable testimony of personal faith in Christ and have publicly identified themselves with Him in Scriptural immersion baptism. When the members of a local church are believers, a oneness in Christ exists, and the members can endeavor to keep the unity of the Spirit in the bond of peace.

Acts 2:41 & 47, *"Then they that gladly received his word were baptized: and the same day there were added unto them about three thousand souls. Praising God, and having favor with all the people. And the Lord added to the church daily such as should be saved."*

For questions, comments, or additional copies of this book, please contact us:

✉ **WRITE**   Remnant Ministries
c/o Caleb Garraway
215 S. Marion Avenue
Washington, IA 52353

☎ **CALL**   917.412.0059

 EMAIL   remnantministriesonline@gmail.com

 GO ONLINE   www.remnantministriesonline.com

ABOUT THE AUTHOR

Caleb Garraway was born into a Christian home on July 20, 1986, and was born into the family of God on November 9, 1994. At the age of 11, he was called to preach through the preaching of Dr. Jack Hyles at Pastor's School in Hammond, IN. When he was 16, God called him to enter the field of evangelism. While attending Oklahoma Baptist College, Caleb traveled with the men's singing group for four years and also worked at the Windsor Hills Baptist Church for two years. He entered full-time evangelism in the beginning of 2009.

Caleb and his wife Katie were married on March 20, 2010. They traveled out of Oklahoma City until God providentially lead them to Marion Avenue Baptist Church of Washington, Iowa, in May 2012. After much prayer with Pastor Joseph Brown, Caleb launched *Remnant Ministries.*

Remnant Ministries seeks to stir up the hearts of Christians around the world in two areas: to passionately reach our generation with the Gospel before it's too late and to enthusiastically stand with confidence and conviction upon the principles and precepts of God's Word. To God be the glory, thousands have been saved and touched by the Lord through this ministry.

In January 2014, Caleb teamed with John Hays of the *"Pure Water for All" Foundation* and traveled into the war-torn country of South Sudan for ten days with twenty-two Khlor Gen water purification systems. They witnessed God move in a spectacular and supernatural way. Though they were privileged to give dozens of villages water purification systems that produce clean physical water for entire villages, their ultimate desire was that many would drink of the pure Living Water of Christ. Over 1,200 spiritually thirsty souls accepted God's free gift of salvation!

Caleb has written other books including: *America: A Journey of Faith & Freedom, C. T. Studd: A Voice for God, Drink From This Water, Found Fully Faithful, Her Knight in Shining Armor, Men on Fire, Our Blessed Book,* and *Our Time to Stand.*

On September 20, 2012, the Garraways were blessed of God with their first child, David. They are unapologetically all about the "old-time religion" and Bible-believing Christianity.

400+ PAGES OF DOCUMENTED HISTORY!
Order today from remnantministriesonline.com

The inception of the United States is an incredible tale of how the hand of God was directly involved in the forming of this nation. Unfortunately, today America has forgotten how it was founded.

The Judeo-Christian principles upon which this nation was built are not a matter of personal opinion, but rather are a matter of public record. As President Woodrow Wilson declared: *"America was born a Christian nation. America was born to exemplify that devotion to the elements of righteousness which are derived from the revelations of Holy Scriptures."* **America: A Journey of Faith & Freedom** reveals through documented history how our Founding Fathers' faith in God carried them through the fight for liberty and made their dream of a free nation a reality. Observe with Caleb Garraway how we truly became the United States of America – *"one nation under God, indivisible, with liberty and justice for all."*

"What an eye opener for all who call themselves Americans! A timely message at a time of peril. I highly recommend that this book be read by every citizen, especially the next generation, and used in every Christian school of America."

– *Hershel "Woody" Williams*
Last living WWII Marine Medal of Honor recipient

Also available from Remnant Publishing

Our Blessed Book
by Caleb Garraway

Our Blessed Book looks into various proofs of Divine inspiration, the process of preservation, the history of the King James Bible and why it is the Word of God for English-speaking people, and the fallacies and corruptions in the new translations.

(190 pages, paperback)

Her Knight In Shining Armor
by Caleb Garraway

Her Knight in Shining Armor is a challenge to young men to retain the principles of character and chivalry, to remain pure in an impure world, and to rely upon God that He will provide for each of them the custom-made helpmeet they need.

(140 pages, paperback)

Remnant Publishing presents easy-to-read **PAMPHLETS!**

KATIE GARRAWAY WRITES TO *young ladies*

Let God Write Your Love Story
by Katie Garraway

Waiting is not easy, especially for Christian young women in this day and age. In *Let God Write Your Love Story*, Katie Garraway shares her story which shows that waiting is worth it. She encourages young ladies to let God be in control of their dreams. Because she has found that God writes the best love stories! *(42 pages, paperback)*

Modesty: An Issue Of The Heart
by Katie Garraway

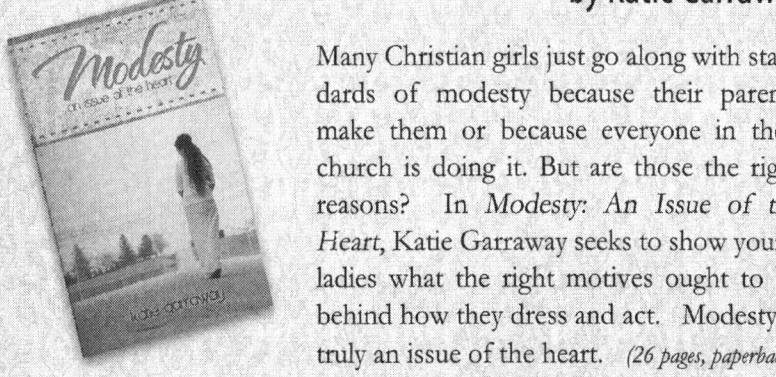

Many Christian girls just go along with standards of modesty because their parents make them or because everyone in their church is doing it. But are those the right reasons? In *Modesty: An Issue of the Heart*, Katie Garraway seeks to show young ladies what the right motives ought to be behind how they dress and act. Modesty is truly an issue of the heart. *(26 pages, paperback)*

VOICES OF Yesteryear

VOICES OF YESTERYEAR, hosted by Evangelist CALEB GARRAWAY, is a great dramatization for anyone who has a burning desire to have God's power upon their life. This one-of-a-kind album features biographical sketches and actual audio clips from the following great men of the past: D. L. Moody, Ira Sankey, R. A. Torrey, Charles M. Alexander, J. Wilber Chapman, Billy Sunday, Homer Rodeheaver, Harry Ironside, Mel Trotter, Bob Jones, Sr., John R. Rice, Jack Hyles, and Evangelist Joe Boyd! As you hear about these great preachers from yesteryear, you will find your heart yearning for personal revival.

This is a recording about men who put a premium on having a walk with God and being filled with the Holy Spirit. In a time when so much in Christianity is watered down, it is refreshing to hear something that takes us back to our old-fashioned roots again.

BE PREPARED FOR 2+ HOURS OF SOUL-STIRRING REVIVAL!